FIFE COUNCIL LIBRARIES

D1353440

Complete
CAT BREEDS

Complete
CAT BREEDS

a comprehensive guide to the most popular breeds of cat around the world

ALAN EDWARDS

veterinary consultant TREVOR TURNER B. VET., M.R.C.V.S.

southwater

FIFE COUNCIL	
219082	
FARR	26/11/01
636.8 EDW	£8.95
NATU	RH

This edition is published by Southwater

Distributed in the UK by
The Manning Partnership
251–253 London Road East
Batheaston
Bath BA1 7RL
tel. 01225 852 727
fax 01225 852 852

Published in the USA by
Anness Publishing Inc.
27 West 20th Street
Suite 504
New York,
NY 10011
fax 212 807 6813

Distributed in Canada by
General Publishing
895 Don Mills Road
400–402 Park Centre
Toronto, Ontario M3C 1W3
tel. 416 445 3333
fax 416 445 5991

Distributed in Australia by
Sandstone Publishing
Unit 1, 360 Norton Street
Leichhardt
New South Wales 2040
tel. 02 9560 7888
fax 02 9560 7488

All rights reserved. No part of this publication may be reproduced, stored in a retrieval system, or transmitted in any way or by any means, electronic, mechanical, photocopying, recording or otherwise, without the prior written permission of the copyright holder.

Southwater is an imprint of Anness Publishing Limited
Hermes House, 88–89 Blackfriars Road, London SE1 8HA
tel. 020 7401 2077; fax 020 7633 9499

© Anness Publishing Limited 2001

Publisher Joanna Lorenz
Managing Editor Judith Simons
Project Editor Mariano Kälfors
Designer Michael Morey
Jacket Designer DW Design
Production Controller Yolande Denny
Editorial Reader Diane Ashmore
Indexer Richard Raper

Previously published as part of a larger compendium, *The Ultimate Encyclopedia of Cats, Cat Breeds and Cat Care*.

1 3 5 7 9 10 8 6 4 2

PICTURE CREDITS
All photography by John Daniels unless otherwise stated.
Animals Unlimited: 8; 10 bl, br; 13 b; 14 c, b; 15 t, c; 16 t, bl; 17 t; 19 t, b; 20 b; 21 t; 37c; 45 b; 46 c, b; 48 c, t; 72 b; 79 t; 81 t; 93 t; b; 96 t; 97 t, b; 98 t; 101 c; 115; 116 bl; 117 t; 118 t, b; 120 b; 123 b; 124 t.
Gilly Cameron Cooper: 116 c, br; 120 cr; 122 t; 123 t.
Chanan Photography, C.A.: 27 t, bl; 49 b; 51; 52–3 all; 55 b; 59 t; 85 c, b; 86 t, tr, b; 87 tl, tr; 116 t; 120 cl; 125 c, b.
FLPA: 10 t; 11 t; 14 t; 22; 40; 51; 54 b; 55 t; 78 t, b; 87 b; 88 t; 90; 105 b; 124 b.
Marc Henrie: 15 b; 16 cl, br; 17 b; 18 b; 27 br; 38b; 47c; 55 t, c; 60 b; 81 b; 92 t, b; 94; 110 t; 111 t; 113 bl; 117 b.
Warren Photographic: 100 b; 101 b; 106; 109 t, b; 110 bl.

Contents

Introduction

Cats have lived with humans throughout most of civilization, but it is only in the last hundred years or so that they have been specifically selected and mated to produce distinct breeds. Unlike dogs, which have evolved over thousands of years and have been bred for almost as long for hunting – with correspondingly wide

Chocolate Tabby Persian

differences in size, shape and character – domestic cat breeds cover a much narrower range of size and conformation, coat type and other characteristics.

Red Birman

WHAT IS A PEDIGREE?
For a cat to be described as a pedigree simply means that its parents have been known and traced back over several generations, and that a written record has been made of this ancestry. A Persian cat of immaculate Persian ancestry could be mated to an equally purebred Siamese. The resulting kittens would be pedigrees, but they would not be classified as a new Persian/Siamese breed until consistent

and healthy litters had been produced for a number of generations (the number may be three or more, depending on the rules and standards of the registering body). Until breed status is attained, purebred cats can only be shown in an "any other variety" category, if at all.

How the many breeds are classified varies with individual cat fancies, even those in the same country. Some of the cats featured in this book are considered to be different breeds in some countries, but as colour varieties of the same breed in others. Within the Persian or Siamese breeds are established colours or coat patterns

Colourpointed Ragdoll Blue

that may have gained official recognition as breeds in their own right, such as the Black Persian or Seal Point Siamese, while the Silver-shaded Burmilla is simply a colour variety of the Burmilla breed. Some breeds or varieties have identical ancestry but have different names or classifications in Britain, continental Europe and the United States – the British Tabby Point Balinese is equivalent to the American Lynx Point Javanese, while the continental Europeans give the name Javanese to the British Angora! Others, such as the Tiffany/Tiffanie have similar names but are unrelated. Attention has been drawn to such anomalies where appropriate. If it all seems rather confusing, do not worry.

More important is to look through the following pages to see the wonderful range of cats available. We highlight the essential features and characteristics of each breed or variety, so that you can find the one that appeals to you and that is compatible with your own lifestyle and personality.

Lilac Tortie Point Balinese

THE FUR FACTOR
We have divided the cat types into Longhair (Persian), Semi-longhair, and Shorthair groups, although for judging purposes, longhairs and semi-longhairs are often combined. Longhaired cats of Persian type are more demanding as

Spotted Tabby Oriental Shorthair

far as grooming is concerned – their long, soft hair needs to be regularly combed and brushed by the owner. However, all the Persians are placid, dignified animals, very glamorous, and well-suited to a predominantly or wholly indoor life. Most of the shorthaired cats, on the other hand, need little or no help with grooming unless they are going to a show. They tend to be more active and playful by nature than the Persians, and need an owner and lifestyle to match. Semi-longhaired cats cover the middle ground between these two extremes, in that their coats need some attention, but not as much as the longhairs. Their personalities depend on their ancestry. Some are longhaired versions of shorthaired breeds, such as the Somali (a semi-longhaired Abyssinian), which has the energetic and playful characteristics of its Abyssinian parentage. Norwegian Forest and Maine Coon breeds have the cold-weather coats and outdoors personalities of their tough, working domestic ancestors.

Black Tortie Tabby Sphynx

Within each grouping, the breeds and varieties are listed in order of importance – relating to how long they have been established and how well-known they are. Some, such as the Exotic Shorthair (Exotic) are strategically placed because of their relationship to other breeds – in this case, the Exotic is a shorthair of Persian type and is found at the beginning of the Shorthair section.

GENE POOL BENEFITS

The great advantage of having a pedigreed and recognized breed is that the outcome of a purebred mating is predictable. Although, depending on the make-up of the ancestral gene pool, there may be colour variations within a litter, the type will be consistent. If you decide to breed from your Maine Coon Cat, you will have Maine Coon kittens. The outcome of a domestic non-pedigreed mating is more of a lottery. The individual breeds and varieties are described according to the ideal standards of perfection set by the various cat fancies. Again, these vary from country to country. An American cat fancy, for example, may prefer a tortoiseshell to have well-defined patches of colour, whereas a European equivalent may like the colours to mingle. Such details are important if you wish to show your cat successfully, and to know what the ideal is may help you select a kitten from a litter. However, many a purebred cat falls short of the official view of perfection, but may still have much of the beauty, grace and temperament of its ancestral heritage.

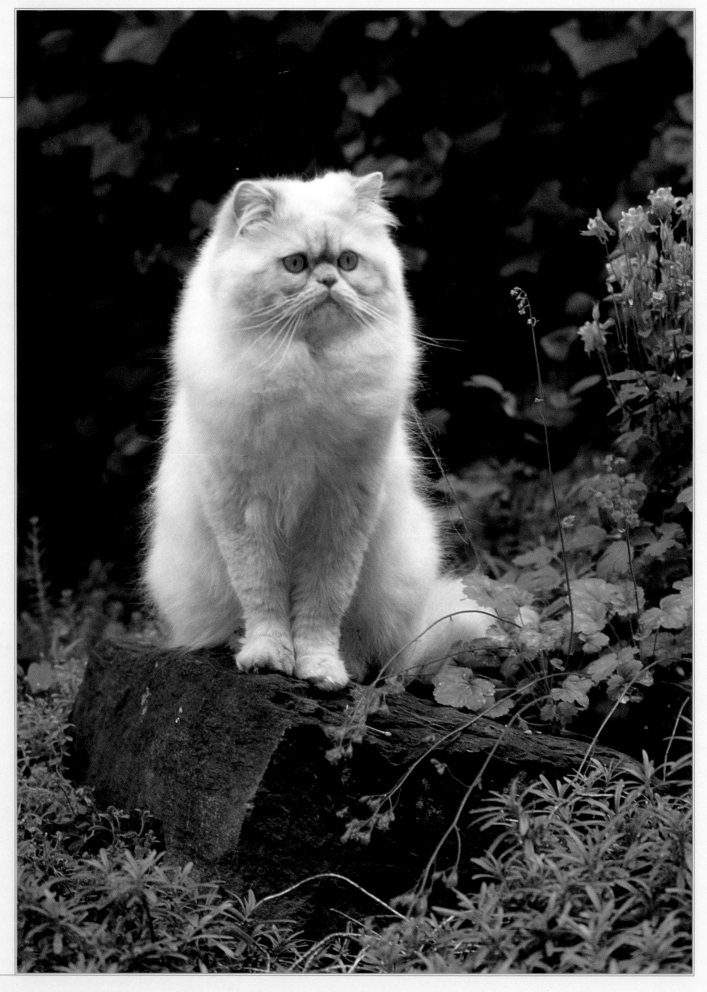

The Longhair Group

The fur of longhair cats can be up to ten times longer than that of a shorthair. Most pedigreed longhair cats are the various types of Persian. They were probably the result of mating early types of Angora cats from Ankara in Turkey with the original Persian cats from what is now Iran. The longhair coat has an underlying layer of soft hairs topped by longer, coarser guardhairs. Although many longhairs are fastidious about their grooming, they need extra help from their owner on a daily basis, even if they are not going to be entered for shows. Another consideration for potential owners is that longhairs tend to moult all year round, leaving fur on carpets and furniture. A contented, well-cared-for longhair cat, however, will bring a glamorous and dignified feline presence into your life.

♦ FACING PAGE
A Supreme Grand Champion displays all the glamour and distinctive features of the classic longhaired pedigree. Champion Rosjoy Rambo is a Cream Colourpoint Persian that won the overall best cat award in Britain's Supreme Cat Show.

♦ LEFT
The Tortoiseshell and White Persian shows off its voluptuous longhaired coat.

THE PERSIAN CAT

All Persian cats – known officially as Longhair Persian type – have the same basic physical shape and conformation. Their faces are flat with short noses and small ears. Their bodies are broad-chested with sturdy legs and large paws, and they all have a soft, thick fur coat with a distinctive ruff around the neck, and a full, low-slung tail. Persian longhairs come in many different colours and patterns. In some countries, such as the United States, the colour variations are considered as varieties of the same breed, but in Britain, each different colour is listed as a separate breed. Persian cats are among the longest-known pedigreed cats. Longhaired variations of wild species may have spontaneously occurred in colder regions in the heart of Asia, and then gradually become established with subsequent interbreeding. The ancestors of today's Persians were probably stocky, longhaired grey cats brought to Europe from Persia (now Iran) in the 1600s and silken-haired white Angora cats from Turkey (a different type from the modern Angora breed). Today, there are over 60 different colour variations of the Longhair Persian type.

♦ ABOVE
The Red Colourpoint is one of the newer, patterned varieties of Persian cat, but it has the voluptuous fur and cobby body, the short nose and small ears of the type.

BLACK PERSIAN

Black Self Persians are thought to be one of the earliest Persian breeds to have been officially recognized as long ago as the 1600s. Today, however, they are not at all common. The show standard insists on a solid, dense coal-black coat, with no hint of rustiness, shading, markings or white hairs. Kittens often show some grey or rusting, and if this continues beyond six to eight months, it is not considered acceptable. To maintain its lustrous black coat, the cat needs to be kept in cool, dry surroundings free from direct light. A damp atmosphere and bright sunlight seem to fade the black – one breeder retired her show cat so that it could enjoy the sunshine. Like many Persians, the Blacks are affectionate and dignified, although they have a reputation for being more playful than the White Persian.

BREED BOX	
Coat	thick, lustrous; full frill at neck and shoulders
Eyes	copper or deep orange; rims black
Other features	nose leather and paw pads black
Grooming	demanding; thorough, daily
Temperament	placid

♦ LEFT
A fully mature Black Persian with a superb coat of solid colour, of the right density and length, and striking, deep copper eyes.

♦ ABOVE
A Black kitten shows great promise as a future show cat. Even though a certain amount of rustiness is accepted in kittens, this youngster already has a superb dense black coat.

WHITE

The White Persian owes its purity of coat colour to the native Angora cat from Turkey. Although quite distinct from the modern Angora breeds, the native Turkish cats were prized for their silken coats, and the white varieties were the most highly sought-after of all. They provided the incentive to breed a pure white Persian type by crossing Angoras and Persians in the 1800s. A show standard White Self should be dazzling white and free of marks or shading. Kittens may have coloured hairs on top of the head but these should disappear before they

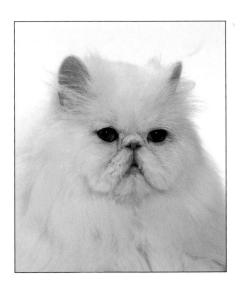

reach the age of nine months. Whites are meticulous self-groomers, but maintaining an immaculate coat is a major challenge for the owner, too. The fur can yellow, especially around the face, legs and tail. However, white grooming powder is available which both cleans and helps guard against staining. The reward for extra effort is a full-flowing, glacial-white coat emphasizing a magical eye colour.

Different varieties of White have been established according to eye colour. Because the original,

BREED BOX

Coat	thick, dense, silky; full frill at neck and shoulders
Eyes	there are three recognized varieties of White Persian: *Blue-eyed White* eyes decidedly blue with deeper shades of blue preferred; rims pink *Orange-eyed White* eyes copper or deep orange; rims pink *Odd-eyed White* one eye blue and one eye orange or deep copper; rims pink
Other features	nose leather and paw pads pink
Grooming	demanding; thorough, daily
Temperament	placid

◆ LEFT
This odd-eyed White with well-defined eye colour probably makes a wonderful companion. However, her ears are too large and set too upright on the head for her to make a perfect pedigreed show cat.

◆ BELOW
An orange-eyed White with everything a judge is looking for. It has a beautifully groomed, luxuriant coat combined with good type.

◆ BELOW
Persian kittens have a woolly coat, without the distinctive ruff around the neck or the fully plumed tail. This one, with its neat ears, cobby body and short face, shows great potential.

blue-eyed variety was prone to deafness (although this is by no means inevitable), it was cross-bred with Blue and Black Persians. The resulting cats were of generally stronger form and build. Some had copper-coloured eyes, others had one orange or copper eye, and one blue eye. The odd-eyed Whites may go deaf in the ear on the blue-eyed side. Whatever the eye colour, both eyes need to be of equal intensity for successful showing.

White Persians are not only glamorous and decorative but happy to be so. Their calm natures make them ideal indoor cats, although they can also be playful.

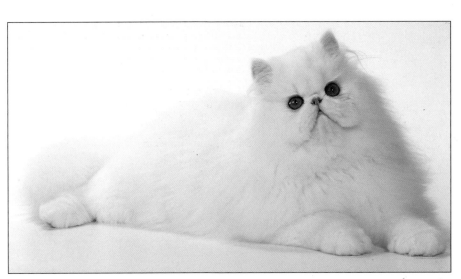

BLUE

At the end of the 1800s, Blue Persians became extremely popular as pets of the wealthy, and were specially bred to be sold for high prices. They became particular favourites of European royalty. Queen Victoria of England acquired two Blues, Princess Victoria of Schleswig-Holstein was an enthusiastic breeder, and King Edward VII presented medals for the top prize-winners of the day.

One reason for the Blue's popularity may have been because it was thought to be the nearest in colour to the original Persians brought to Europe by traders in the 1600s. The genetic mutation of the breed we know today may well have arisen on the Mediterranean island of Malta – which is why it is sometimes called the Maltese Blue. The blue-grey colouring is a dilution of black. The blue comes from a lavender sheen which adds a brightness to the pale coat. This is very much in evidence with the show cat, which is ideally an even, medium to pale blue, with no shading, markings or white hairs. A dark, slate-grey coat is considered very undesirable. Because of its long, distinguished history of careful breeding, the Persian Blue is often used as the standard Persian type against which other Persian breeds are compared. For this reason, it is sometimes included in breeding programmes to improve the type of other varieties.

The Blue has a reputation for being a very affectionate and gentle cat that enjoys close human companionship.

◆ LEFT
The Blue was one of the first Persian cats to be established as a breed. In the late 1800s, it became a fashionable asset for the wealthy and aristocratic.

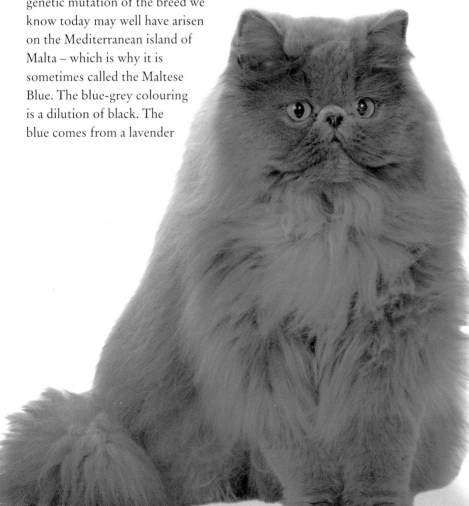

BREED BOX	
Coat	thick, dense, silky; full frill at neck and shoulders
Eyes	copper or deep orange; rims blue-grey
Other features	nose leather and paw pads blue-grey
Grooming	demanding; thorough, daily
Temperament	placid

◆ LEFT
A Blue with a well-earned aristocratic air. Its evenly coloured coat with a lustrous sheen offsets glorious copper-orange eyes.

CHOCOLATE

There is an element of Siamese in the Chocolate Persian, which may account for a certain sauciness in its nature.

The Chocolate Point Siamese was mated with Blue Persian cats to create part of the formula for the Persian Colourpoint. The Chocolate was an offshoot, and gradually, through generations of breeding, it became a recognized variety in its own right. The ideal show cat has a medium to dark, warm and evenly toned coat with no shading, markings or white hairs. Warmth of tone rather than a deep, dark bitter chocolate is very important. Kittens sometimes show greying, although this often disappears at six to nine months. Eyes should be rich copper-orange with no signs of reversion to pale gold or green.

♦ ABOVE
The eyes should be copper-orange. There is a tendency for eye colour to revert to pale gold or even tints of green.

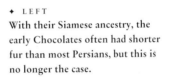

♦ LEFT
With their Siamese ancestry, the early Chocolates often had shorter fur than most Persians, but this is no longer the case.

BREED BOX	
Coat	thick, silky
Eyes	copper or deep orange; rims chocolate brown
Other features	nose leather and paw pads chocolate brown
Grooming	demanding; thorough, daily
Temperament	placid

LILAC

The Lilac Persian, or Lavender Kashmir was, like the Chocolate, an offshoot from the breeding programme for Colourpoint longhairs. It is a dilute form of the Blue with an element of Siamese. This may be the reason why these cats often show an independence of spirit – they are well able to amuse themselves, but quickly bond with their owners.

The perfect pedigree has a thick, silky coat that is warm in tone and even in colour, with no markings or white hairs. Eyes are copper or deep orange with lilac rims, and the nose leather and paw pads are also lilac. Once the colour Lilac has been produced, Lilac to Lilac matings will only produce Lilac kittens. This applies not only to Persian Lilacs, but to other breeds as well, with the exception of Oriental Shorthair Siamese and British Shorthair breeds.

♦ RIGHT
A Lilac Persian has a coat colour that is warm and even, with no shading.

BREED BOX	
Coat	thick, silky
Eyes	copper or deep orange; rims lilac
Other features	nose leather and paw pads lilac
Grooming	demanding; thorough, daily
Temperament	placid

RED

♦ LEFT
Here is a face full of character, but judges would probably be looking for a shorter nose. Some shading on the head is acceptable, but tabby markings should not be obvious in mature cats.

Only a few decades ago, the Red Persian was one of the rarest of all feline varieties. This was largely because of the need to select parents which had had fine mackerel-striped coats as kittens, combined with long fur and intensity of colour. The fiery red coat is much richer than that of the ordinary ginger tom. For a show cat, it should be even in tone, with no white hairs. Slight shading on the forehead and legs is acceptable. The sex-linked gene which creates the red cannot mask the tabby markings that are characteristic of all Red Persian kittens in certain lights. It is rare for a Red to be free of these markings until the ground colour has intensified with maturity.

BREED BOX	
Coat	thick, silky
Eyes	copper or deep orange; rims deep pink
Other features	nose leather and paw pads deep pink
Grooming	demanding; thorough, daily
Temperament	placid with spark

♦ RIGHT
It is common for Persians to moult in the summer months, resulting in loss of top coat due to the heat. This lovely example of a Red still shows good type despite being what is known as "out of coat".

CREAM

The Cream Persian is a dilute Red, with probable input from the white Angoras that were cross-bred with Persians in the 1800s. Then, as now, Blue Persians were not only the most popular variety, but the best examples of type, so breeders of other colours used Blue studs in their programmes. Blues are dilutes of Black Persians, and so dilute genes were released into many breeding programmes, eventually resulting in a whole range of dilute colours.

Early Creams had larger ears and longer noses than their modern descendants, and their eyes were almond-shaped. Today's Cream is the result of over a century of very selective breeding that was initially done in America. The English described these dilute Reds as "spoiled oranges", and did not regard them as an acceptable colour variation until the 1920s. The ideal Cream has no shading, markings or white hairs. The pale to medium cream coat is even in colour with no white undercoat.

BREED BOX	
Coat	thick, silky
Eyes	copper or deep orange; rims pink
Other features	nose leather and paw pads pink
Grooming	demanding; thorough, daily
Temperament	placid

♦ RIGHT
A Cream kitten is particularly precious as some breeders think that this variety has smaller litters than other Longhairs.

TORTOISESHELL

The classic Tortoiseshell colouring is a striking blend of black, red and pale red. The exact configuration of colours is very much influenced by the mix of colour genes carried by the female parent. If the female gene has two red XX chromosomes, the offspring will be red. However, if one of the female's chromosomes carries the red gene and one does not, then the offspring will be a mixture of red and another colour or colours – a Tortoiseshell. Because of the complex genetic make-up necessary to create the Tortoiseshell mix of colours, all variations are usually female.

Tortoiseshells, also known as Torties, occur in dilute variations, such as Chocolate Tortie, Blue-Cream and Lilac-Cream. The parentage is reflected in the names.

The object in breeding any Tortoiseshell pedigree is to achieve a perfect balance in the mix of colours. When black and chocolate are intermingled with red, the result can be a brilliant firework display of a coat. Aficionados of these varieties hope that the colours will be well-defined, and better still, that the kittens will

♦ RIGHT
A Black Tortoiseshell shows off its fine cobby build, with solid, squarish body, short, thick legs and large head. Because Tortoiseshells have been cross-bred with a good mixture of other breeds, they tend to show excellent type.

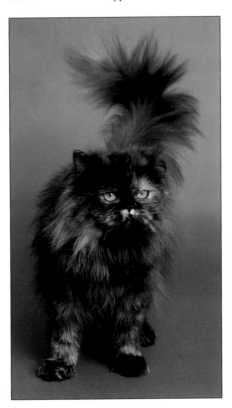

♦ ABOVE
This Black Tortoiseshell is differently marked from the one at the top of the page. Tortoiseshells come in several colours, although a mix of red or cream patches on the base coat colour are desirable. No two Tortoiseshells are ever the same.

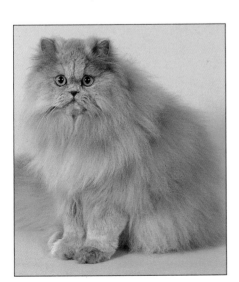

♦ LEFT
The Blue-Cream is a subtly coloured Tortoiseshell which arose from crossing a Blue Persian with a Cream. The American and English standards differ. The English like the two colours to merge, while the Americans prefer distinctive bands of blue and cream.

have a dashing blaze of red down the centre of the face. Some kittens show greying in the black fur, which usually grows out after six to nine months.

Tortoiseshells with red in their make-up are said to inherit the allegedly fiery temperament of the Red Persian, though their fans say they are just full of character. They also tend to be particularly attentive mothers. Tortoiseshell queens are mated with Blacks and Reds for the best chance of producing Tortoiseshell kittens in their litter.

The ethereal colour of the dilute Tortoiseshells is said to be complemented by a certain charm and winsomeness of character. According to the British standard, the soft colours should merge into each other like shot silk. In America, distinct bands of colour are preferred.

Eyes of all Tortoiseshells are large, full and deep copper or orange.

BREED BOX	
Coat	thick, silky
Eyes	deep orange or copper
Other features	nose leather and paw pads pink or black, depending on dominant coat colour
Grooming	demanding; thorough, daily
Temperament	placid

BI-COLOUR

In the early days of pedigree breeding, any longhaired cat with a patch of white was regarded with horror. However, there were so few animals without a white spot on the belly or neck, that to fill classes at shows, the Bi-colours were allowed to compete. These solid-coloured cats with white undersides, muzzles, chests, legs and

♦ ABOVE
A Blue Bi-colour is an example of the many variations of the breed. They are available in all the colours accepted for the Self colours such as Red, Cream and Chocolate.

BREED BOX	
Coat	thick, dense, silky; full frill at neck and shoulders
Eyes	deep orange or copper
Grooming	demanding; thorough, daily, especially the white parts
Temperament	placid

♦ LEFT
A beautifully groomed black and white Bi-colour in full coat shows the distinct white patching that is highly desirable in show cats.

feet, were placed along with the Tortoiseshell and Whites, in an "any other variety" category. Eventually, breeders began to consider them seriously as a variety in their own right. The ideal standard is for the white patches to be balanced and even, with a dapper and clearly defined inverted V shape running over the nose.

TORTOISESHELL AND WHITE

The classic Tortoiseshell's black and red (or its dilute colours) are offset by patches of dazzling white – as long as the cat is well and frequently groomed. In America this variety is called a Calico after printed calico (cotton).

♦ BELOW
Tortie and Whites occur in as many different colour combinations as the Tortoiseshells themselves. This is a dilute colour – Blue Tortie (Blue-Cream) and White.

BREED BOX	
Coat	particularly long and silky; full frill at neck and shoulders; full, bushy tail
Eyes	orange or deep copper
Grooming	demanding; thorough, daily, especially the white parts
Temperament	placid

♦ BELOW
A black Tortie and White displays well-mingled markings, clearly defined white patches, and an exceptionally fine longhaired coat.

The English version of this name was Chintz, but this is no longer used. The American standard requires well-defined patches of colour, but in the United Kingdom, any degree of white is acceptable, from some on all four legs, chest and belly, to the van pattern.

TABBY

◆ BELOW
The rich marmalade-coloured coat of the Red Tabby
is marked with deep copper – and the eyes are a
complementary golden orange.

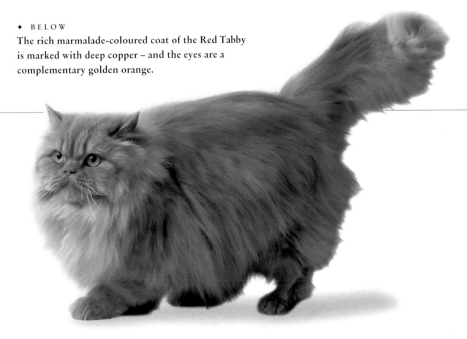

If Tabby Persians were groomed in the exaggerated bouffant style applied to other varieties, the impact of their rich markings would be diminished. Even though a full coat is still important, the Tabby owner has to take a more laid-back approach to grooming.

The characteristic Tabby markings include triple lines running the length of the spine, a butterfly shape over the shoulders and an oyster (or spiral) on the flanks. Legs and tail should have evenly spaced dark rings, and the underbelly is spotted. Spotted, mackerel and ticked tabby patterns are also shown, apart from in the United Kingdom, where the only recognized variations are blotched (or marbled). Mainstream Tabby colours are Brown, Red and Silver, although other varieties such as Cream, Lilac and Cameo are being introduced. The Brown Tabby is rich, tawny-sable ground with dense black markings. It was especially favoured by Frances Simpson, the premier breeder of Blue Persians in the late 1800s. One of her champions became the ancestor of most Brown Tabbies in the world today. Strong types of Tabby from the United States are currently being introduced worldwide.

The Red Tabby, with its rich ginger coat and matching eyes, however, remains the most popular variety. Next in line are the Silvers. They have been subject to dispute over correct eye colour for show cats, especially in the United Kingdom. Elsewhere, a looser interpretation of achievable eye colour has meant that Silver Tabby Persians have now been bred to the very best of type characteristics.

BREED BOX	
Coat	thick, silky, often shorter than other longhair varieties
Eyes	*Brown and Red:* orange or copper with no green rim *Silver:* green or hazel
Other features	*Brown:* nose leather brick-red; paw pads black or brown *Red:* nose and paw pads deep pink *Silver:* nose leather brick-red with black outline; paw pads black
Grooming	demanding; thorough, daily; special care brings out markings
Temperament	placid

◆ ABOVE
Tabbies require careful grooming to enhance distinctive markings like those on this Brown Tabby. As well as his characteristic Tabby M on the forehead, his short nose and ears are perfect.

◆ RIGHT
The scintillating fur colour of the Silver Tabby made it a favourite in early cat shows – until it was upstaged by the silvery Chinchilla.

CHINCHILLA

In 1882, a fine-boned, silver Angora-type female cat with no markings was mated with a similarly coloured, non-pedigreed male. Their daughter became the mother of the

◆ LEFT
When a Chinchilla moves, the coat appears to sparkle, which is why the breed is sometimes described as ethereal or fairy-like.

BREED BOX

Coat	thick and dense, like swansdown
Eyes	emerald or blue-green; visible skin on eyelids black or dark brown
Other features	nose leather brick-red; paw pads black or dark brown
Grooming	demanding; needs constant attention
Temperament	placid; often livelier than other Persians

first Chinchilla title holder, whose body was exhibited in London's Natural History Museum.

The undercoat of the Chinchilla is pure white. The coat on the back, flanks, head, ears and tail is tipped with black. The tipping should be evenly distributed to give the characteristic silver sparkle. The legs may be slightly shaded with the tipping, but the chin, ear furnishings, stomach and chest must be pure white. Tabby markings or brown or cream tinges are undesirable. There has been great controversy about the required size of a Chinchilla;

the breed is sometimes described as fairy-like, but this is not to do with size – Chinchillas are usually medium-sized and quite solidly built.

◆ ABOVE
The Chinchilla's emerald or bluish-green eyes are outlined in black, creating an eyeliner effect.

GOLDEN

Golden cats may well have occurred as an offshoot of Chinchilla breeding in the 1920s. However, the modern breed became established following an explosion of American imports of Chinchillas into Britain in the 1970s, combined with a New Zealand import from American bloodlines. On the back, flanks, head

and tail the undercoat must be sufficiently tipped with seal brown or black to give a golden appearance. An apricot undercoat deepens to gold, while chin, ear furnishings, stomach and chest are pale apricot. The general tipping effect may be darker than that of the Chinchilla, and tipping on the tail may be heavier than on the body. Legs may be shaded, but the back from paw to heel should be solid seal brown or black. Kittens often show tabby markings or grey at the base of the undercoat.

◆ LEFT
The Golden Persian, originally called the Golden Chinchilla, has the same striking dark rims around the eyes.

BREED BOX

Coat	dense, silky
Eyes	emerald or blue-green; eye rims seal-brown or black
Other features	nose leather brick-red outlined with seal or black; paw pads seal or black
Grooming	very demanding; thorough, needs daily attention
Temperament	placid, but often livelier than other Persians

SHADED SILVER

The Shaded Silver is largely the product of Chinchilla matings to self-coloured longhairs in attempts to improve size and type.

The general effect of a Shaded Silver is of being much darker than the Chinchilla. The undercoat is pure white, with black – never blue – tipping that shades down from the back to the flanks, with lighter tipping on the face and legs. The top side of the tail is also tipped, but the chin, chest, stomach, insides of the legs and underside of the tail are pure white. The tipping extends to a third of the complete hair length. The hair on the foot pad to the joint may be shaded to black and there is no barring on the legs. Lips are outlined in black. No tabby markings or brown or cream

BREED BOX	
Coat	thick, dense, silky
Eyes	emerald or blue-green
Other features	nose leather brick-red outlined with black; paw pads black or seal
Grooming	very demanding; thorough, daily
Temperament	placid, but often livelier than other Persians

♦ ABOVE
The darker tipping of the Shaded Silver compared with the Chinchilla is quite clearly seen. The Shaded Silver is derived from Chinchilla cross matings. In Britain it took a long time for it to be recognized.

tinges are permissible in a show cat. In the United States, breeders mated to the best Persians available (Black or Blue) and then inbred to regain the Chinchilla breed features. Shaded Silvers were the inevitable consequence, and throughout the history of Silver Persians in the United States, both Chinchilla and Shaded Silver kittens have been produced in the same litter.

SMOKE

Smoke Persians are the result of cross-breeding Chinchilla, Blue and Black. The traditional Smoke colours are Black and Blue – but the introduction of the red sex-linked gene, followed by the gene for Chocolate, led to the entire range of longhair colours being represented. Black Smokes were the first to be introduced. Blue Smokes were initially kept as pets rather than show cats, because they were considered to be poor-quality Blue Persians.

All Smokes are cats of striking contrasts. The undercoat should be as white as possible, with the tips shading to the appropriate colour. The darker points are most defined on the back, head and feet, and the light points on the frill, flanks and ear tufts.

BREED BOX	
Coat	thick, dense, silky; full frill
Eyes	large, round; orange
Grooming	very demanding; thorough, daily
Temperament	placid

♦ LEFT
Startling orange eyes are offset against the darkest fur colouring of the tipped Persians. The Smoke shows dramatic ash white undercoat contrasting with the full colour.

CAMEO

The Cameo was regarded as a delicious accident for a great many years, but towards the end of the 1950s, the breed was formally registered in the United States. The formula for creating Cameos turned out to be extraordinarily straightforward, with kittens of consistent colouring appearing in the first hybridization.

◆ LEFT
A Persian Red Shell Cameo has fur that is tipped at the very ends to give a shimmering effect.

BREED BOX	
Coat	thick, dense, silky; full frill at neck and shoulders
Eyes	large, round; deep orange or copper
Grooming	demanding; thorough, daily
Temperament	placid

Apart from Red and Cream Cameos, there are Blue-Cream and Tortoiseshell variations.

There are two levels of colour tipping to the fur. In the Shell Cameo, colour is restricted to the very tips of the fur to give a soft sheen like mother-of-pearl. The Shaded Cameo has heavier tipping, and normally occurs in the first crosses between a Chinchilla and a Red or Cream cat. In all Cameos, the undercoat should ideally be as white as possible with the tips shading to red or tortoiseshell in the Red series, and shading to cream or blue-cream in the Cream series. The deepest intensity of colour is most defined on the mask, along the spine from the head to the tip of the tail and on legs and feet. The light points occur on the frill, flanks, undersides and ear furnishings.

PEWTER

Breeding from Tortie Cameos produces cats with black rather than red, cream or tortoiseshell tipping. These cats are a relatively recent development and have their place as

BREED BOX	
Coat	thick, long; full frill
Eyes	deep orange or copper
Other features	nose leather and paw pads brick-red
Grooming	thorough, daily
Temperament	placid

Pewters. They are very similar in appearance to Shaded Silvers but with orange or copper eye colour. Pewters are recognized in the United Kingdom only with black tipping. The coat is exceptionally long – almost to the point of obscuring the cobby build – with a full neck ruff ending in a frill over the front legs.

◆ ABOVE
Orange-copper eyes distinguish the Pewter from the similar Shaded Silver Persian. This cat's distinguished neck ruff descends satisfyingly deep to finish between the front legs.

COLOURPOINT (HIMALAYAN)

The entire catalogue of Persian longhaired cats until this point has been based on a solid colour cat modified by the introduction of the tabby pattern, sex-linked colour, silver or white patching. The pioneers of Colourpoint breeding fused the Persian type longhair with the Himalayan (which is why this breed is known in America as Himalayan) pattern of the Siamese cat. The result was a cat of Persian type with long hair and the restricted coat pattern of the Siamese. The points (mask, legs, feet and tail) are evenly coloured and there is a good contrast between the points and body colour. Light body shading, if present, should be confined to the shoulders and flanks, and should complement the points. The mask covers the entire face. It should not extend over the head, although the mask of a mature male is more extensive than that of a mature female. Kittens are born white and fluffy, the point colours starting to appear in less than a week.

Attempts to transfer the Siamese pattern to Persian type were being made before World War II, but the cats were not shown until 1957 in California, and were only officially incorporated into the Persian breed by the Cat Fanciers' Association in 1984. Breeding lines have since expanded to develop the full range of point colours. The Colourpoint Persian has now outstripped the Blue in the longhair popularity stakes.

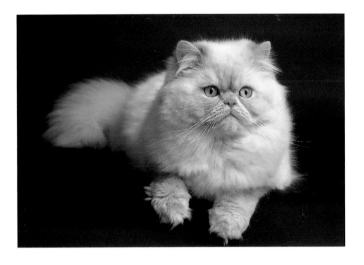

♦ LEFT
Cream Colourpoint
Rosjoy Rambo,
Supreme Grand
Champion, has the
wonderful blue eyes
of a Siamese set
against the red-gold
cream of his fur.

POINT COLOURS

Individual organizations recognize point colours that include the Silver series and Red sex-linked Silver series. In Britain, the point colours are represented by four distinct groupings:
Solid point colours – Seal, Blue, Chocolate, Lilac, Red and Cream
Tortie point colours – Seal Tortie, Blue-Cream, Chocolate Tortie and Lilac-Cream
Tabby point colours – Seal Tabby, Blue Tabby, Chocolate Tabby, Lilac Tabby, Red Tabby, and Cream Tabby
Tortie Tabby point colours – Seal Tortie Tabby, Blue-Cream Tabby, Chocolate Tortie Tabby and Lilac-Cream Tabby

In the United States, seven varieties are recognized:
Blue Point, Chocolate Point, Seal Point, Flame Point, Lilac Point, Blue-Cream Point, and Tortoiseshell Point

BREED BOX

Coat	thick, dense, no trace of woolliness; glossy; full frill over shoulders and continuing between front legs
Eyes	large, round; brilliant blue
Other features	nose and paw pad colour matches the point colour
Grooming	demanding; thorough, daily
Temperament	placid

♦ BELOW
The darkened points of the Siamese are blended with all the characteristics of the Persian Longhair. This cat is a Blue Colourpoint.

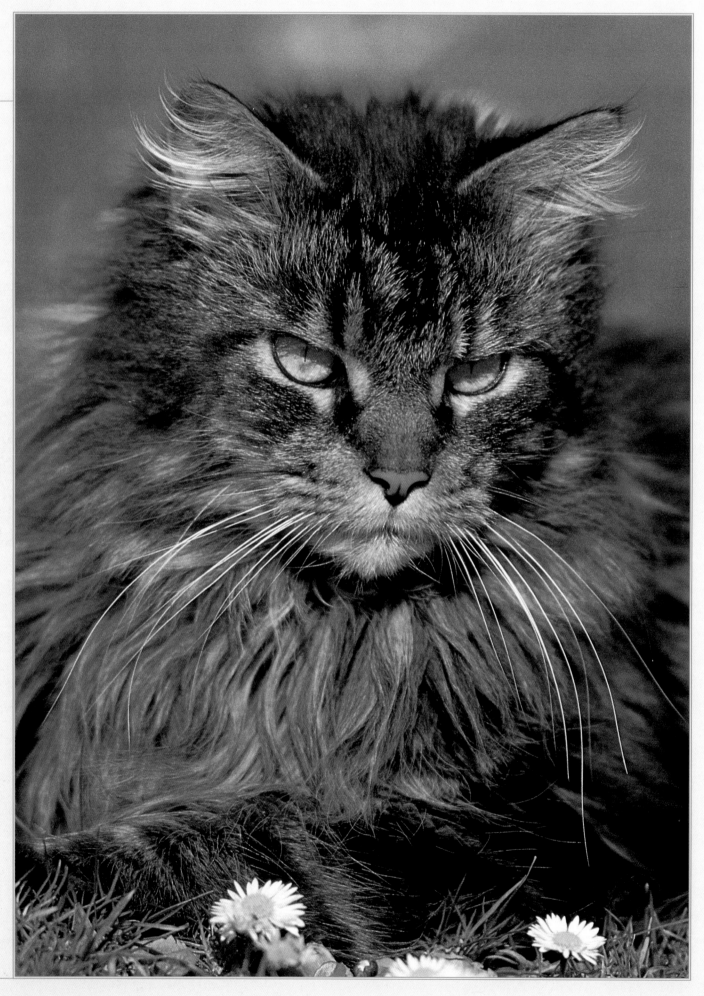

The Semi-longhair Group

Many semi-longhair breeds, such as the Norwegian Forest Cat, are of natural ancestral type; others, such as the Ragdoll and the Somali, are relatively new "manufactured" breeds.

In each semi-longhair breed, the coat seems to have a distinct pattern of growth that is like no other. However, in its fullest expression – in the Maine Coon Cat, for example – there are the common features of lynx-like ear tufts, inner ear furnishings and a chest ruff which can reach right down between the front legs. Coats can be rather shorter over the main part of the body but there is a drift of fur on the flanks and "breeches" on the back legs. Paws often show tufts between the toes under the paws, and tails are long and plume-like.

◆ FACING PAGE
Some of the semi-longhair breeds have developed coats that provide protection against hard winters; the Maine Coon Cat is one.

◆ ABOVE
Semi-longhair versions of shorthaired breeds have been developed. This Blue Somali is like an Abyssinian apart from its longer coat.

BIRMAN

◆ LEFT
The pale coat and coloured points on face, legs
and tail are similar to those of a Siamese cat.
However, this Blue shows the distinctive white
paws that are unique to Birmans.

The Birman falls somewhere between
the Siamese and the Persian in its
character, build and length of fur, yet
it is very much a breed of its own. It
also has the distinction of being the
sacred cat of Burma.

All Birmans have colourpointed
features – darker coloration on the
ears, face, tail and legs. The original
Birman was seal-pointed, but there are
now blue, lilac, chocolate, and a wide
range of tortoiseshell and tabby
points. All are now regarded as
different breeds, but share the same
blue eyes, dark points, white feet,
body shape and general temperament.

The Birman body has some of
the mass of the Persian's, with thick-
set legs and a broad, rounded head.
However, the body and legs are longer
than those of a Persian, and the face is

pointed rather than flat, with a longish,
straight nose and relatively large ears.

The unique and most distinctive
feature of the Birman is its paw design.
Each forepaw ends in a symmetrically
shaped, white glove. The show

BREED BOX	
Coat	long, silky; full ruff around the neck and slightly curled on the stomach
Eyes	almost round but not bold; deep, clear blue
Other features	white mittens on forepaws; longer white "gauntlets" on rear paws
Grooming	relatively easy with regular brushing and combing
Temperament	gentle, individualistic, extremely loyal

◆ BELOW
The mask, tail and legs of Seal
Point Birmans take their colour
from the rich brown of Burmese
soil, according to one legend.

◆ RIGHT
The Seal Point original has now
been joined by many differently
coloured varieties of the Birman,
but all have clear sapphire eyes
and a sweet facial expression.

standard is for the white to end in an
even line across the paw and not pass
beyond the angle of paw and leg. The
white areas on the back paws taper up
the back of the leg to finish just below
the hock, and are known as gauntlets.
These white finishing touches are the
result of a rare recessive genetic trait,
although, rather more romantically,
there are various legends that explain

The Red Point Birman has a cream body colour with warm orange points, the trademark white paws, but pink nose and paw pads.

their origins. One version tells of a raid on a Burmese temple in which the high priest was killed. A white temple cat leapt on to the priest's body, and immediately its fur turned gold in the light radiating from the resident goddess. The cat's eyes reflected the sapphire of the goddess's own eyes, while legs and tail took on the rich brown of the Burmese soil. The paws that rested on the dead priest, though, remained white, a symbol of purity.

A more recent story reports that in 1919, a pair of seal-pointed Birmans was given to French explorer August Pavie and Englishman Major Gordon Russell. The male died on the journey back to France, but the female survived and bore a litter. This queen may have represented the beginning of controlled breeding of Birmans in France during the 1920s, when Siamese and bi-colour Persians were introduced into the programme. The breed was officially recognized in 1925. Its character reflects the Persian and Siamese input. It is quieter and less active than the Siamese, but not as docile as the Persian. The queens mature earlier than a Persian – at around seven months – and are generally very attentive mothers.

◆ RIGHT
The Chocolate Tabby Birman, one of the newer colours, shows pale chocolate tabby markings on ears, mask and tail, while the body is light golden beige.

BIRMAN POINT COLOURS

Seal, Blue, Chocolate, Lilac, Red, Cream

Tortoiseshell points in all colours apart from Red and Cream

◆ RIGHT
A Blue Tortie Tabby Point displays a magnificent coat and tail. A Birman's coat needs some extra grooming, but is less demanding than that of a longhair breed, and rarely becomes matted.

TURKISH VAN

◆ RIGHT
A classically coloured auburn and white Turkish Van – this one has the unique distinction of winning the United Kingdom's Supreme Cat Show two years running.

Ancestors of the Turkish Van come from a rugged region in south-east Turkey, around the country's largest lake, the 3675km² (1419 square mile) Lake Van. This may be why this breed apparently loves water – and is sometimes called the Turkish swimming cat. It is not true that all cats hate water, but these cats will actually seek it out and seem to swim as a form of recreation. Turkey's domestic cats are predominantly white with auburn markings. Even today, in Istanbul, you will see many street cats of this colouring.

On a visit to the Lake Van region in the 1950s, two English women bought a stocky white female cat with flashes of head colour and a full auburn tail.

◆ ABOVE
The "thumbprint" markings on the head of this auburn and white Van correctly (for the show standard cat) do not extend below the eyeline.

Their Istanbul hotel manager told them of another cat – a male with very similar markings. They took both cats back to Britain, and after four years were successfully breeding consistently patterned kittens. The two women returned to Turkey and bought another male and female to add to the new gene pool. The breed was first officially recognized in Britain in 1969 as the Turkish Cat, the name later being changed to Turkish Van.

Despite its fine coat and white colouring, no link with the Turkish Angora breed has been established. The Van is the more muscular of the two breeds, deep-chested with a long, sturdy body. Its legs are medium in length with neat, tufted, well-rounded feet. The tail is a *pièce de résistance*, a full brush in perfect proportion to the body and, of course, coloured and possibly faintly ringed. The cat has a long, straight nose and prominent, well-feathered ears.

The perfect coat is chalk-white with no trace of yellow, with coloured tail and head markings not extending below the eye line or the base of the ears at the back. There is a white blaze on the forehead and sometimes the occasional thumb-print of colour on the body. All colours are recognized (auburn and cream only in the United Kingdom).

Turkish Vans have reached the height of excellence, including the title of Supreme Exhibit at the United Kingdom's Supreme Cat Show.

BREED BOX

Coat	long, soft, silky; no woolly undercoat
Eyes	large, oval, expressive; light to medium amber, blue or odd-eyed
Other features	enjoys swimming; not prolific (litters of about four kittens)
Grooming	relatively easy; daily brushing and combing
Temperament	affectionate, intelligent; not particularly lively; may be nervous

◆ LEFT
The creamy-white Turkish Van is one of the two colours accepted by the United Kingdom's cat fancy, the other being the classic auburn and white.

TURKISH ANGORA

When the Victorians launched their breeding programmes using longhaired Persians and white cats from Ankara in Turkey, the Persian type became dominant. While the Turkish cat was an essential ingredient in the creation of the longhaired Persian of today, its type did not catch on to the same extent as the Persian. The result was that by the early 1900s, there were no Turkish Angoras on the international show scene and the type was nearly wiped out. However, it has always been highly valued in its land of origin, and a handful of cats was kept at Ankara Zoo. They continued to breed there in relative obscurity until rediscovered by the rest of the world in 1963. A pair was taken to America and a breeding programme started, although it is still not recognized by the main United Kingdom cat fancy. The white version, in particular, is now

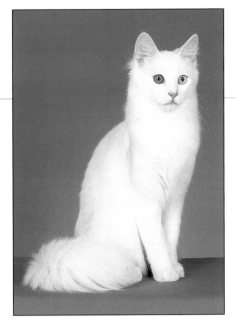

◆ ABOVE
The pure white Turkish Angora is probably the closest to the first longhaired cat that was brought to Europe from Ankara, Turkey in the 1500s. This one, however, is a highly bred odd-eyed white with a definitely modern form.

◆ BELOW RIGHT
The Turkish Angora's pert and pretty profile and splendid plume of tail can be appreciated on this Black Tortie Smoke.

BREED BOX

Coat	fine, silky, medium length; wavy on stomach; no undercoat
Eyes	large, almond shaped; amber, blue, odd-eyed; green for Silver cats
Other features	moults heavily in summer
Grooming	relatively easy; daily brushing and combing
Temperament	affectionate, intelligent, can be playful; enjoys peace and quiet

highly prized in its native Turkey. The Turkish Angora is a graceful, small to medium-sized cat, with a neat and attractively tapered head. To begin with, only the white versions were recognized but now there is a whole range of selfs, bi-colours, tabbies and smokes.

◆ ABOVE
A Calico Turkish Angora shows the alert expression and high-set ears typical of the breed.

SOMALI

◆ LEFT
An example of the Usual – or original colour – with an undercoat overlaid with rich golden brown and each hair tipped with black.

The Somali is the semi-longhaired version of the Abyssinian cat. Although the Abyssinian is a shorthaired breed, semi-longhaired kittens have occasionally appeared in their litters over several decades. In the United States it was eventually realized that a new breed was appearing spontaneously. The long fur was the result of a naturally long-established recessive gene within the breeding population. It may have been introduced via ticked tabby cats of unknown parentage in the breeding programme. These cats would have been introduced to sustain the breeding viability of the early Abyssinians, for the gene pool was extremely restricted at the turn of the century – a state of affairs that lasted well into the 1920s and 1930s. Any

connections, the breed was named after the nearby African country of Somalia.

The coat pattern of the Somali is quite distinctive: it is ticked – with three two-colour bands of colour on each hair. The colour combinations now bred range from the traditional,

BREED BOX	
Coat	soft, fine, dense; lies flat along the spine
Eyes	almond-shaped, slanting; outlined with a darker surround; amber, hazel or green, the richer and deeper the better
Other features	smiling expression
Grooming	easy if done regularly
Temperament	intelligent, lively, alert, interested; may be shy; freedom-loving (must not be confined indoors)

◆ LEFT
The Sorrel Somali is rather paler than the Usual as the base apricot is ticked with cinnamon rather than black.

fluffy Abyssinian kittens were initially regarded as below standard and banished to pet homes. Then an American breeder discovered that a longhaired Abyssinian at a humane society home had actually been sired by her own stud cat. The stud was tried out again to see if a consistent line of semi-longhairs could be produced – and the Somalis were established during the 1960s. Because of its Abyssinian or Ethiopian

◆ RIGHT
While the adult (*left*) shows full colouring, it is not uncommon for a kitten (*right*) to show greyish roots, and this is quite acceptable if you are showing a youngster.

◆ LEFT
The Blue Somali is attractively marked in a soft
blue overlying a pale mushroom undercoat.

◆ LEFT
In recent years, silver variations of the breed
have been introduced. This Fawn Silver Somali
(silver undercoat ticked with fawn) is quite rare.

SOMALI COLOURS AND PATTERNS

Usual	rich gold-brown, apricot ticked with black
Sorrel	apricot ticked with cinnamon
Chocolate	apricot ticked with dark brown
Blue	mushroom ticked with blue
Lilac	mushroom ticked with lilac
Fawn	mushroom ticked with fawn

Also Red, Cream, six Tortie
colours and Silver versions of all
these colours

◆ ABOVE
The Somali's foreign ancestry is evident in its
pointed face and almond-shaped, slanting eyes.
Ideally, the eyes are beautifully defined by a
dark outline surrounded by a ring of light fur.

◆ BELOW
With its fur lying flat along the back, the coat
of the Somali should be distinctly longer
around the neck, hindquarters and on the
tail – as this Blue Silver shows.

or Usual, (Black) and
Sorrel (Cinnamon)
to Blue, Chocolate, Lilac,
Fawn, Red, and Cream.
There are also Tortoiseshell
and Silver variations.

The ideal Somali is a
beautifully balanced cat of
medium build. Its body is firm,
lithe and muscular with long legs
and a long, bushy tail. It has tufts
of fur between its toes. Ears are
tufted, too, and are set wide apart,
prominent and pricked. The
head is slightly pointed and
well-contoured.

Although not quite as outgoing
as its Abyssinian relations, the
Somali is not a cat that is
suited to being confined
indoors. It is a charming
and striking animal, with
a bright-eyed, alert and
fox-like cheeky
demeanour.

MAINE COON CAT

The Maine Coon Cat is a fine working cat, as well as one of the longest established breeds. As the first part of its name suggests, it comes from Maine, America's most north-easterly state. This is a land of mountains, forests, lakes and inhospitable winters.

BREED BOX

Coat	thick, dense, waterproof; has an undercoat
Eyes	full, round with a slightly oblique aperture; all colours (including blue and odd-eyed in white cats)
Other features	big; good climbers; smallish litters (two or three kittens)
Grooming	coat rarely gets matted but regular brushing and combing advised
Temperament	intelligent, calm; freedom-loving (should not be confined indoors)

♦ LEFT
The Brown Tabby is the traditional Maine Coon Cat pattern. Individuals may take three or four years to reach the size and stature of this one.

The Maine Coon Cat is appropriately powerfully built, with an all-weather coat and a reputation for being a wise and skilful hunter.

The second part of its name comes from the long tail and density of fur that have been compared to the similar attributes of the raccoon, an indigenous North American mammal. Like the raccoon, the cat is an exceptional climber. Another theory suggests that the lynx-like tufts on many a Maine Coon's ears are a result of genes inherited from the North American lynx, but this is unlikely. It is more likely that there is a touch of Angora in the breed. Local cats could have bred with Angoras that landed with sailors at the East Coast ports,

or, less plausibly, with the cats sent to America by the French queen Marie Antoinette to escape the French Revolution. (The queen did do this, but it is unlikely that her animals founded a new race of cats.) It may

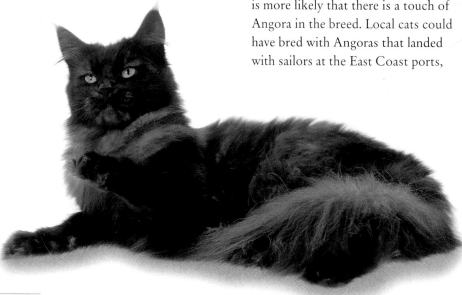

♦ ABOVE
A Blue Maine Coon Cat shows the ideal head shape and feathered ears typical of the breed. It was once suggested that the ears were inherited from the North American lynx.

♦ LEFT
A black mantle overlays a paler root colour on the Smoke Maine Coon Cat. The fur is generally shorter over the head and shoulders and lengthens down the back and sides.

simply be that the domestic cats which travelled from Britain to North America with the Pilgrims way back in the 1600s were the true source of Maine Coon Cats, and that the breed's long coat evolved as protection against the severe Maine winters.

The Maine Coon Cat is not only one of the longest established breeds in the world, but also one of the largest. It can weigh 9kg (20lb) and more, compared with an average 2.5–5.5kg (5–12lb) range. Its history rivals that of many more fashionable breeds, and it now has an international following to match. It is the second most popular pedigreed cat in the United States after the Persian. This was not always so.

It was one of the earliest exhibition cats – on show in New York in 1860 and in country shows and fairs in New England. Its early popularity was reversed when there was a craze for the more exotic Persians and Siamese being imported into the United States in the early 1900s. It was not until the 1950s that Maine Coon Cats slowly began to creep back into favour, and it was accepted at championship level in 1976. Now they are found all over the world with the current top American lines taking the highest honours.

Despite its size, the Maine Coon Cat is a gracious animal, with full cheeks and high cheek-bones, a square muzzle and a firm chin. Its nose is slightly concave in profile. Ears are large, set high and wide apart. The body is long of back, culminating in a very long, bushy tail that tapers at the tip and is carried high and proud. Legs and paws are substantial.

Recently, rexed (curly coated) kittens have been born to apparently purebred Maine Coon Cats in the United Kingdom, indicating that behind some of the pedigrees, a rexed cat has been knowingly or unwittingly introduced. The variation is not approved of by the clubs and associations monitoring the Maine Coon Cat breed. Every attempt is being made to eliminate the gene.

✦ LEFT
Beneath the thick overcoat of the Maine Coon Cat is a solid, muscular body that has all the necessary power for a working cat.

MAINE COON CAT COLOURS AND PATTERNS

Solid	White, Black, Blue, Red, Cream
Tabby and Tortoiseshell	all colours in classic and mackerel patterns, including Silver variations

Also occurs in shaded, smoke, bi-colour, tortoiseshell and white, and van bi-colour. Only one-third white preferred in patched cats

✦ BELOW
A softly coloured Red Silver and White shows paler colouring on chest and paws.

✦ ABOVE
A Tortoiseshell Tabby and White has the required large, oval eyes of the breed, a nose of medium length, and a splendid set of whiskers.

NORWEGIAN FOREST CAT

The Norwegian Forest Cat has been described as the "kissing cousin" of the Maine Coon Cat. The land it comes from certainly has similarities to the forested mountains of Maine. The Norwegian Forest Cat also originated as a natural outdoor working cat, on Scandinavian farms, and its powerful build and skill as a climber and hunter reflect this heritage. Its double-layered coat is heavier during winter, and keeps out both cold and wet. The generous frill and "shirt front" of fur of the neck and chest may be shed during the summer months.

Although it is a big, strong-legged animal, the Norwegian Forest Cat has a certain elegance. Its head is triangular with a long, straight profile, and ears are pointed, open and erect. Like the Maine Coon Cat, it matures slowly and may not reach full stature until four years of age. All colours are allowed except Chocolate, Lilac and

Colourpoint (Himalayan) pattern. The Norwegian Forest Cat is one of the semi-longhaired varieties that have developed as a northern hemisphere speciality. Whether it goes as far back as the Vikings – who describe a "fairy cat" in their legends – is unknown. However, the Vikings travelled not only to the shores of the Mediterranean, and along the rivers

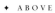

✦ ABOVE
The Norwegian Brown Tabby has the breed's characteristic stance, with a slightly raised rump, and the long, plumed tail raised high.

NORWEGIAN FOREST COLOURS AND PATTERNS

Solid	White, Black, Blue, Red, Cream
Tabby and Tortoiseshell	all colours in classic and mackerel patterns, including Silver variations

Also occurs in shaded, smoke, bi-colour, tortoiseshell and white

✦ LEFT
This Silver Tabby is in full winter coat, with a splendidly well-furnished ruff and "shirt front".

A Black Norwegian Forest Cat demonstrates the breed's typical smooth outer layer of fur that covers a warm, woolly undercoat.

of Asia, but also to the East Coast of North America. It is entirely feasible that the warrior-traders could have found longhaired Asian cats such as the Angora from Turkey, and taken them back to Scandinavia, and even, perhaps, on to America. The Norwegian Forest Cat may therefore quite possibly share the same rootstock as the Maine Coon Cat, its North American equivalent.

By the 1930s the Norwegian Forest Cat was being taken seriously by pedigreed cat lovers in Norway, and it featured at the foundation of Norway's oldest cat club in 1938. However, it only attained full championship status from FIFe, Europe's main feline organization, in 1977, and in the United States in 1993.

✦ LEFT
A Blue Bi-colour displays the distinctively long feathering from the ears, and big, slightly obliquely set eyes. There should be extra points for the splendid whiskers, too!

BREED BOX

Coat	thick; double coat – a woolly undercoat covered by a smooth, water-repellent overcoat; thick ruff
Eyes	large, round; all colours
Grooming	easy; occasional combing
Temperament	alert, active; loves people; freedom-loving (must not be confined indoors); enjoys rock and tree climbing

✦ RIGHT
Norse legends refer to a "fairy cat", and the subtle colours, softness of line and pretty face of this Silver Tortoiseshell Tabby certainly have an ethereal quality.

BALINESE (JAVANESE)

Imagine a Siamese cat with a long, silky, flowing coat and a feathered tail, and you have an idea of the Balinese. It has the same dazzling sapphire eyes and large, erect ears as the Siamese cat – and comes in the same colour variations. However, the Balinese – or Javanese as some colours are called in the United States – tends to be a little less noisy than the Siamese.

Its names are probably inspired by the cat's graceful movement that is reminiscent of an Indonesian dancer. (Further confusion, however, arises because in Europe, the Javanese is the name given to what the British call the Angora!) The ancestry, however, is certainly Siamese. It is likely that in over 100 years of breeding Siamese cats, the recessive gene for long hair crept in and, in the 1940s, longhaired kittens began to appear in purebred Siamese litters. A Californian breeder decided to take advantage of this tendency, and in the 1950s developed a fully constituted pedigree breed. The new breed was introduced to the United Kingdom and Europe in the 1970s. Soon, some remarkably beautiful animals were being bred.

The fur of the Balinese is shorter than that of many of the other semi-longhairs, and lies

◆ ABOVE
Balinese cats are found in all the same point colours as the Siamese. This Blue Point shows how the longer fur of the Balinese can have the effect of making a subtler transition between points and main body colour.

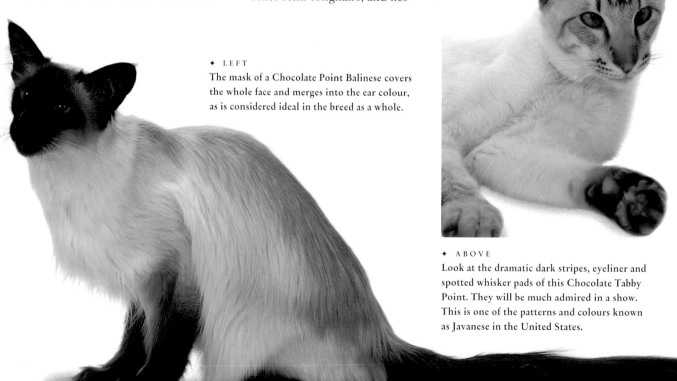

◆ LEFT
The mask of a Chocolate Point Balinese covers the whole face and merges into the ear colour, as is considered ideal in the breed as a whole.

◆ ABOVE
Look at the dramatic dark stripes, eyeliner and spotted whisker pads of this Chocolate Tabby Point. They will be much admired in a show. This is one of the patterns and colours known as Javanese in the United States.

BREED BOX

Coat	medium length, fine, silky; lies mainly flat along the body; no woolly undercoat
Eyes	almond-shaped, slanted; alert, intelligent expression; clear brilliant blue
Other features	feathered tail
Grooming	relatively easy; regular gentle brushing and combing
Temperament	intelligent, lively, playful, loyal, affectionate but can be aloof

smooth over the body. The cat is consequently easier to maintain. It is of medium build, but long-limbed and lithe, with the distinctly wedge-shaped head and long, straight nose of the Siamese. The mask is complete over the face and linked to the ears by traces of the darker colour (except in kittens). In character, the Balinese is bright and very active but loves its comfort.

◆ **RIGHT**
Bright clear eyes of intense sapphire blue like those of this Chocolate Point are a scintillating feature of the breed.

◆ **LEFT**
Perfectly balanced shading along the spine of this Lilac Point tones in beautifully with a magnolia body colour and the darker points, but ideally there should be no shading at all.

◆ **ABOVE**
Vocal, yes, but the Balinese may not be as loud nor as raucous as its Siamese ancestors.

BALINESE/JAVANESE POINT COLOUR GROUPS

Seal, Blue, Chocolate, Lilac (Frost), Red, Cream

Tabby, Tortoiseshell Tabby

Seal Tortie, Blue Tortie, Chocolate Tortie, Lilac Tortie

ANGORA

This Angora is not to be confused with the Turkish Angora. It is the semi-longhaired variety of the Oriental Shorthair. It has the temperament, body structure and elegance of the Oriental cats, including a tendency towards loud and persistent vocals. They have inherited this from the Siamese element in their breeding programme. The breed was created in Britain from a mating between a Siamese and a Sorrel Abyssinian which carried the longhair gene.

Angoras are lithe and balanced of body with the long legs and almond eyes of their Oriental ancestry, and similarly quick of mind, playful and affectionate. The long, fine coat does not reach its peak until the cat is fully mature. Then its tendency to be wavy and ruffle up at the neck and chin can conceal the fine-boned muscularity of the body beneath, but this is easily felt when you stroke the fur smooth.

The Angora is bred in all standard solid colours, tortoiseshell, tabby, smoke and shaded varieties, but not colourpointed or bi-colour.

◆ ABOVE
The abundance of silken fur on the Cinnamon Angora's underside can conceal the svelte body that lies beneath.

◆ RIGHT
The Oriental lineage of this Chocolate Angora is apparent in its wide-set, almond eyes and wedge-shaped face.

◆ RIGHT
From the large, erect ears along a fine, long nose, this Fawn Angora's head seems to converge in a triangle to a neat, strong chin.

BREED BOX

Coat	fine, silky, medium length; smooth apart from ruffling at chin, neck and belly; no woolly undercoat
Eyes	large, wide-set, almond-shaped; green, apart from blue- and odd-eyed whites
Other features	tufted ears; long, tapering, plumed tail
Grooming	relatively easy; regular brushing and combing
Temperament	intelligent, lively, inquisitive, active, need company

RAGDOLL

When a Ragdoll is picked up it is supposed to go limp – and that is how it came to be named. There is a far-fetched story that the first Ragdoll kittens are said to have inherited this characteristic, together with an apparent resistance to pain, because their white semi-longhair mother, Josephine, had been injured in a road accident. It is more likely that the Ragdoll's docile nature arises from a happy coincidence of character genes. The breed was created in California in 1963. An early alternative name was Cherubim, while some variations are called Ragamuffins. Although the original breeder claimed non-pedigreed parentage, it is likely that Birman and Burmese genes were present somewhere along the line. However, in the majority of cats the dominant white spotting gene creates the look of the Mitted variety, while the one that produces a similar effect in the Birman is recessive.

The Ragdoll is a cat of powerful build, with big, round paws and a long, bushy tail. Its head is broad and wide-cheeked with a slightly retroussé nose

◆ **BELOW**
A Seal Colourpointed Ragdoll has distinct, deep brown points.

◆ **ABOVE**
A Blue Colourpointed gives a good overall impression of the breed's solid, powerful build. Colourpoints have the traditional pattern of complete coloured mask, ears, legs and tail.

BREED BOX	
Coat	dense, silky
Eyes	small, round, slanted; deep blue
Other features	goes limp when picked up
Grooming	easy; daily brushing with soft brush
Temperament	docile, relaxed, easy to handle; needs calm (so suitable to confine indoors)

and wide eyes of deep sapphire . The three recognized main groupings are: Colourpointed, Mitted and Bi-colour. The Mitted has Colourpointed features contrasting with a pale body, plus white-gloved front feet and rear legs white to the hock or beyond. The Bi-colour is white on the chin, bib, chest and underbody with a triangular blaze over its nose.

◆ **LEFT**
White gloves on the forepaws and longer gauntlets on the rear legs are the distinctive features of the Mitted Ragdoll and bear witness to the probable Birman genes in the breeding programme.

◆ **ABOVE**
A triangular nose blaze denotes the true look of the Bi-colour Ragdoll. Bib, chest, underbody and front legs are also white.

TIFFANIE

The Tiffanie is a semi-longhaired version of the Asian group of shorthaired cats. It was developed in the United Kingdom during the 1980s and is only just beginning to establish itself as a breed. Burmilla cats featured strongly in the original breeding programme, with occasional injections of Burmese to strengthen the type. The result is that this pretty cat is now found in all the colours and patterns found in the Burmese and Asian breeds. It is a medium-sized cat, although the females tend to be smaller than the males and are particularly dainty. Ears are set wide

◆ LEFT
The Tiffanie's Asian roots are evident in the large, wide-set, slightly oriental, and very expressive eyes of this Blue Shaded Silver.

BREED BOX

Coat	fine, silky; pronounced ruff and tail plume
Eyes	slanted; gold to green; green preferred in the Silver variations; gold allowed in self colours
Grooming	relatively easy; regular brushing with soft brush
Temperament	stable, dignified, but inquisitive · and sociable

apart, angled slightly forward, and quite large in relation to the head; ear tufts are common. The head, rounded at the top, tapers slightly through butterfly wing-effect cheeks to a

firm chin. It is fairly similar in appearance to a breed that was initially developed as the Tiffany in North America. In 1967, a pair of chocolate-coloured, semi-longhaired cats with gold eyes and unknown parentage, produced a litter of six identical kittens and a breeding programme

TIFFANIE COLOURS AND PATTERNS

Self colours	Black, Blue, Chocolate, Lilac, Red, Caramel, Apricot, Cream
Tabby and Tortoiseshell	Black, Cream, Blue, Chocolate, including Silver versions. The Tabby patterns are less defined on the semi-longhair coat than on the Asian shorthaired equivalent

◆ RIGHT
The British Tiffanie, a recent addition to the show circuit, is now found in an enormous range of colours and patterns, as this Brown Smoke version suggests.

◆ BELOW
A Brown Shaded Silver Tiffanie shows excellent shape, with a perfectly straight back from shoulder to hindquarters, and a soft, feathery tail.

began. However, no Burmese were included in the programme, nor were ever produced in any subsequent litter. The colour and pattern range of the breed was increased during the 1980s, and it is becoming more common. The name has been registered as Chantilly/Tiffany to avoid confusion with the British Tiffanie.

CYMRIC

The Cymric is the longhaired version of the Manx cat. A clear standard of points has been prepared in the United States. The variety is not recognized in the United Kingdom.

The Cymric (which means of, or from, Wales) was inevitable as far as genetic inheritance is concerned, even though the longhair gene is recessive to the shorthair gene. It was necessary

to introduce tailed outcrosses into Manx breeding programmes to strengthen the type. This widened the gene pool and so increased the possibility of the recessive longhair gene finding a match and producing a longhaired version of the Manx cat.

The first recorded Cymric appeared in Canada in the 1960s and the variety gained impetus from that point,

mainly in North America. As with the Manx, there is the "true" rumpy version with a hollow in place of a tail, the stumpy – with a stub of a tail, and the occasional long-tailed version. The rumpy's lack of tail is caused by a mutant gene similar to the one that causes spina bifida in humans, and kittens born to cats with this condition may be stillborn.

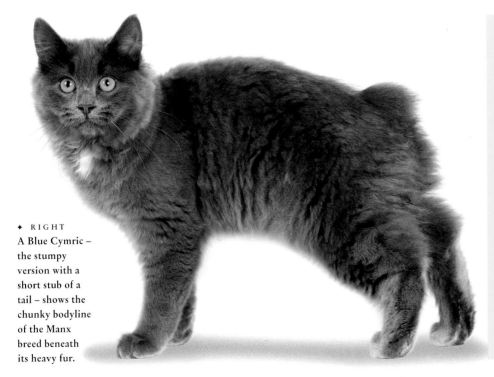

◆ RIGHT
A Blue Cymric – the stumpy version with a short stub of a tail – shows the chunky bodyline of the Manx breed beneath its heavy fur.

BREED BOX	
Coat	silky with hard guardhairs; not cottony, uneven in length
Eyes	large and round; colour in keeping with coat colour
Other features	may have no tail, a stump or a nearly full tail
Grooming	easy with daily brushing
Temperament	affectionate, intelligent, extremely loyal; likes to be with its owner

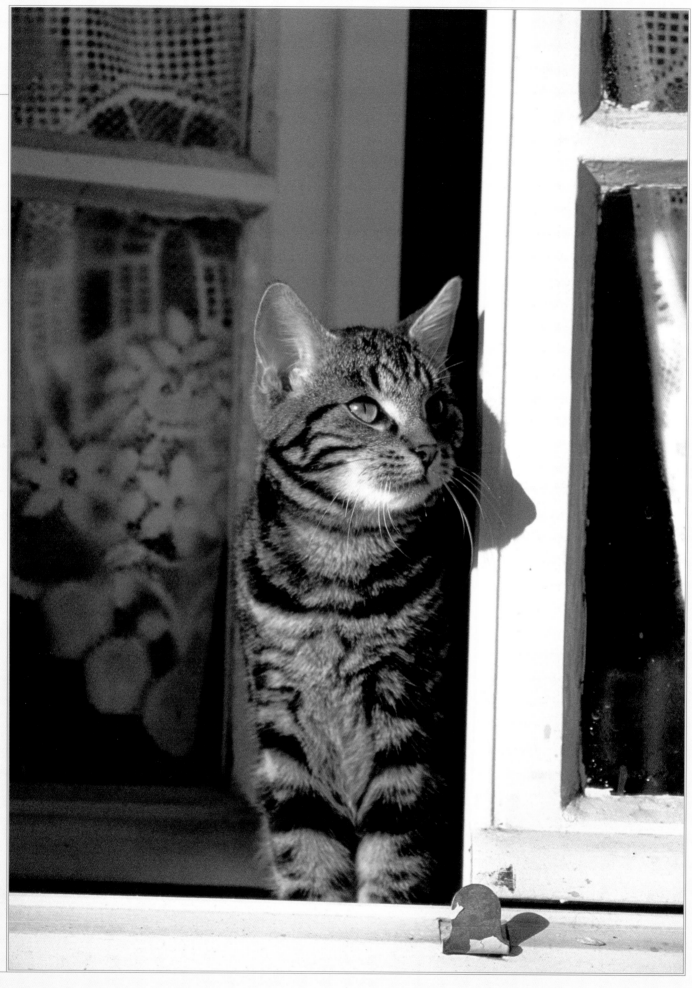

The Shorthair Group

Most cats, whether pedigrees or non-pedigrees, are shorthaired like their wild ancestors. Short hair is not only more practical for a wild hunting cat, but also for the domestic animal and its owner. Domestic shorthairs tend to be much more independent and agile than the longhairs, and their body shape can be appreciated. They also need little or no grooming and any wounds can be easily seen and tended. Shorthaired pedigreed cats have been bred into perfect examples of their type from indigenous domestic cats. They fall into two main groups – the sturdy, round-faced American, British and European shorthairs and the long-limbed, lean-featured cats of Asia.

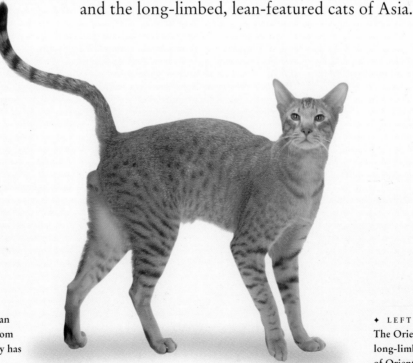

◆ FACING PAGE
A European Tabby Shorthair is an example of a breed developed from indigenous feral cats. It probably has a long and impressive pedigree.

◆ LEFT
The Oriental Spotted Tabby is a long-limbed, lean-featured shorthair of Oriental origin.

EXOTIC SHORTHAIR

The aim in breeding the Exotic Shorthair (known simply as the Exotic in the United States) was to produce a Persian cat without the long hair to reduce the grooming commitment. These shorthaired cats are judged in the Longhair Persian-type section, which can cause some confusion for newcomers to the showing scene.

In facial make-up and expression, body shape and even character, the Exotic Shorthair has all the characteristics of the Persian breeds, and is even available in the same colours and variations. It is a medium-sized cat with a short body, short, thick legs and large paws. The head is round, with a short nose and small, wide-set, round-tipped ears. Breeders

◆ ABOVE
Brilliant orbs of gold-copper are startling against the solid density of the Black Exotic Shorthair. The nose leather and paw pads are black.

BREED BOX

Coat	medium, slightly longer than other shorthairs, but not long enough to flow; dense, plush, soft, full of life; not flat or close-lying
Eyes	large, round, bright; colour reflects coat colour
Other features	small, blunt ears, set wide apart and leaning slightly forward
Grooming	easy; thorough, daily brushing and combing
Temperament	gentle, affectionate, good-natured, inquisitive, playful

◆ ABOVE
Eyes complement the rich red of the Red Tabby's coat. Brilliance of eye colour is an important distinction for this breed in general.

◆ BELOW
A Silver Tabby shows off her eyes lined in black like a Chinchilla. Her shorter coat, however, appears more darkly tipped and the pattern more obvious than that of the longhaired Shaded Silver.

◆ LEFT
The coat of a Blue-Cream Exotic shows definite, but scattered areas of cream among the subtle shades of soft blue-grey.

◆ BELOW
A Tortoiseshell Colourpointed Exotic demonstrates the distinctive Persian body conformation with the large, round head, full body and shortish tail and legs.

of British Shorthairs maintained a policy for a long time of outcrossing to Persian cats every fourth generation or so. They wanted to encourage massiveness of bone and intensity of eye colour in the existing breed, rather than create a new one. Persian type was not, in fact, very distant from the British Shorthair and was therefore likely to improve it.

American breeders, however, did not have a large gene pool of British Shorthairs. They therefore used the Burmese (which was the one really round-headed cat they did have), and later the American Shorthair. The way in which the American cat fancy had developed the Burmese from its introduction in the early 1930s had ensured that its head shape and eye shape were closer than any other breed to Persian Longhair type. This meant it was only a matter of a few generations of kittens before the Exotic Shorthair was successfully developed in the 1960s. Since 1968, Burmese and British Shorthairs have

not been allowed in Exotic breeding programmes in the United States.

It soon became popular, and is now bred in the full range of self colours, bi-colours, tabbies and tortoiseshells, and shaded, tipped and colourpointed varieties. Judging standards are very stringent, with an emphasis on brilliance of eye colour. Any hint of slanted eye shape from the Burmese contribution to its lineage, or a fleck of rogue colour in the iris is frowned

upon. The Exotic Shorthair has the placidity and dignity of the Persian, yet has a playful and affectionate side. It is patient with children, and is contented to be an indoor cat.

Despite being shorthaired, the coat is longer than other shorthaired breeds and requires more attention. It benefits from daily grooming. Try brushing or combing from tail to head, against the pile of the fur to encourage the fur to stand up, brush-like, from the body.

◆ ABOVE
Persian facial features combine with the blue eyes of colourpointed varieties in this Tortoiseshell Colourpointed Exotic. The colourpointed range is fully represented in the breed.

◆ RIGHT
A Tortoiseshell and White Exotic has the required rich tones of red set among the dense black base colour. The red blaze on the face is a bonus.

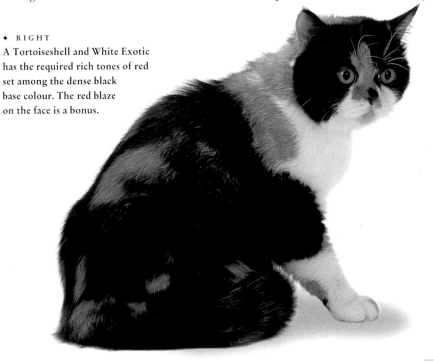

THE BRITISH SHORTHAIR

The national cat of the British Isles, the British Shorthair, is the result of selective breeding of the best examples of native street cats. It probably stems originally from the first domestic cats that arrived in Britain with the Roman legions in the first century AD. As a pedigreed variety, the British Shorthair (or the English Cat) was recognized from the very start. The early breeders of British shorthaired cats, were, for some reason, usually male and from the north of England. Now the British Shorthair is the third largest group of registered pedigreed cats in the United Kingdom and popular throughout the world.

It is bred in all the major colour and pattern groups, although to a lesser extent than the American Shorthair, and includes a Siamese pattern. All British Shorthairs have a compact, well-balanced and powerful body. The chest is full and broad; legs are short and strong with large, rounded paws; the tail is thick at the base and rounded at the tip. Of the British, European and American Shorthairs, the British has the most rounded head. The ears are small and set wide apart, the cheeks are round, the chin firm, and the nose short and broad.

Like its non-pedigreed ancestors and contemporaries, the British Shorthair is a streetwise, muscular cat whose characteristic placidity enables it to adapt happily to life indoors. Its intelligent yet phlegmatic nature makes it a solid and dependable feline companion.

BRITISH BLACK

All the essential characteristics of the British Shorthair type are often seen at their peak in the Black. This is because it was one of the earliest British Shorthair breeds to be selectively bred from the very best of British street cats in the 1800s. It was also one of the first to be shown at the first national cat show in 1871 at Crystal Palace, London.

The top-rate pedigreed Black should have a dense black coat from hair root to tip, with no hint of browning, stray white hairs, patches or tabby markings. This provides a striking backdrop for the large, round, deep copper eyes with absolutely no green.

Blacks are often used in breeding programmes to improve the type of other Shorthair breeds, particularly Tortoiseshell and Tortie and White.

BREED BOX

Coat	short, thick, fine
Eyes	round; copper, no green
Other features	round-tipped ears; short nose; big round paws; nose leather and paw pads black
Grooming	easy; regular combing
Temperament	companionable, independent, freedom-loving

◆ LEFT
The densely coloured, short fur of the British Black Shorthair is inherited from ancestors reputed to be the familiars of witches, and the butt of superstition and legend during the Dark Ages and medieval times.

BRITISH WHITE

Pure white condensed into the stocky build of the British Shorthair is the epitome of feline luxury and perfection. British White Shorthairs are universally admired, highly valued, and quite rare, although they have been bred since the 1800s.

There are three varieties with different eye colours. Blue-eyed Whites may rarely be prone to deafness. In trying to breed out this defect by crossing with orange-eyed cats, an odd-eyed variety with one eye of each colour was created. Unfortunately, these cats sometimes suffer deafness in the ear on the blue-eyed side. Orange-eyed varieties are therefore the most commonly seen.

BREED BOX	
Coat	short, thick, fine
Eyes	round; clear blue, orange to copper, or one of each
Other features	round-tipped ears; short nose; big round paws; nose leather and paw pads pink
Grooming	easy; regular combing
Temperament	companionable, independent, freedom-loving

◆ ABOVE
A British White Shorthair with a pristine coat is hard to breed and therefore not very common. A pure white non-pedigree might look very like a pedigreed shorthair, but it is more likely to have green eyes rather than copper, blue, or one of each colour.

BRITISH CREAM

The occasional occurrence of a cream-coloured kitten in tortoiseshell litters towards the end of the 1800s provided the motivation to try to produce a Cream pedigree. Some tortoiseshell parentage is necessary to produce the required rich shade of buttermilk, which made it difficult to produce consistently pale coats with no redness or obvious tabby markings.

The result was that the breed was not officially recognized until the 1920s and not fully established until the 1950s. Sometimes tabby markings become more pronounced in very hot or very cold weather. The ideal is cream-haired to the roots – with no patches of white.

BREED BOX	
Coat	short, thick, fine
Eyes	round; deep gold to orange and copper
Other features	round-tipped ears; short nose; big round paws; nose leather and paw pads pink
Grooming	easy; regular combing
Temperament	companionable, independent, freedom-loving

◆ LEFT
British Cream Grand Champion, Miletree Owain Glyndwr, has only the faintest shadow of darker markings, and a gloriously soft-toned coat colour.

BRITISH BLUE

The Blue is the most popular of British Shorthair breeds. Kittens often display tabby markings, but these usually disappear after six to eight months. Because the breed is long established, from the earliest programmes in the 1800s, Blues tend to be good examples of the Shorthair type: broad, muscular and good-natured. Occasional injections of black

✦ ABOVE
A round-cheeked British Blue's hazy blue-grey coat contrasts with big orange eyes.

shorthairs and blue longhairs into breeding programmes have preserved the distinctive slate-blue coat.

BREED BOX	
Coat	short, thick, fine
Eyes	round; copper, orange or deep gold
Other features	round-tipped ears; short nose; big round paws; nose leather and paw pads blue-grey
Grooming	easy; regular combing
Temperament	companionable, independent, freedom-loving

BRITISH CHOCOLATE

The warm, dark-chocolate coloration comes from the introduction of the chocolate gene from longhaired colourpoints into the British Shorthair breeding programme. The coat can be any shade of rich chocolate but it should be evenly toned, without any white, shading or marking.

✦ RIGHT
Despite the British Shorthair's reputation for being stolid and reliable, this Chocolate shows the lively intelligence for which the breeds are also known.

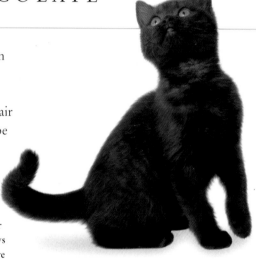

BREED BOX	
Coat	short, thick, fine
Eyes	round; deep gold, orange to copper
Other features	round-tipped ears; short nose; big round paws; nose leather and paw pads brown or pink
Grooming	easy; regular combing
Temperament	companionable, independent, freedom-loving

BRITISH LILAC

✦ BELOW
The stocky, muscular build that distinguishes the British Shorthair from its European and American counterparts can be clearly seen in this Lilac.

The Lilac, a soft-toned blue-grey with a pinkish sheen to it, is a recently introduced, dilute form of the Chocolate. The gene responsible for the dilution produces hairs in which the pigmentation is collected together in clumps, and microscopic areas of hair have no pigment at all. The dilute colour therefore has less depth and intensity than a pure solid colour. Lilac parents only produce kittens of the same colour, unless they carry cinnamon, so once established, Lilacs are easy to keep on producing.

BREED BOX	
Coat	short, thick, fine
Eyes	round; rich gold to orange or copper
Other features	round-tipped ears; short nose; big round paws; nose leather and paw pads pale grey
Grooming	easy; regular combing
Temperament	companionable, independent, freedom-loving

BRITISH BI-COLOUR

◆ BELOW LEFT
The mask over the ears and three-quarters of the face that is such an important feature in the show Bi-colour, suits the rounded features of the British Shorthair very well.

There are many bi-coloured cats on the streets of Britain, but the pedigree version must have well-balanced, symmetrical and clearly defined bands 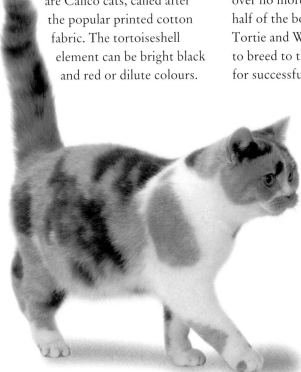 of solid colour and white. The coloured areas can be black, blue, red, cream, chocolate or lilac and in the perfect pedigree, contain no flecks of other colours or any tabby markings. It is also important for the show cat to have the white area covering the nose and lower part of the face, neck and shoulders, chest and forepaws – but over no more than half of the total body area.

BREED BOX	
Coat	short, thick, fine
Eyes	round; gold to orange and copper
Other features	round-tipped ears; short nose; big round paws; nose leather and paw pads pink
Grooming	easy; regular combing
Temperament	companionable, independent, freedom-loving

BRITISH TORTIE AND WHITE

This variation of the Bi-colour has tortoiseshell in place of the solid colour areas. In America, these are Calico cats, called after the popular printed cotton fabric. The tortoiseshell element can be bright black and red or dilute colours.

As with the solid colour and white, the white areas should extend over no more than half of the body. Tortie and Whites are quite difficult to breed to the preferred symmetry for successful showing.

◆ ABOVE RIGHT
British Shorthairs also come in tortoiseshell without white in mingled shades of red and black, as shown, or the dilute blue-cream shades.

◆ LEFT
The Tortie and White Shorthair comes in delightful dilute versions such as this softly dappled Blue Tortie and White.

BREED BOX	
Coat	short, thick, fine
Eyes	round; orange to copper
Other features	round-tipped ears; short nose; big round paws; nose leather and paw pads pink and/or black
Grooming	easy; regular combing
Temperament	companionable, independent, freedom-loving

BRITISH TABBY

The tabby gene is a forceful one, passed on from the wild species from which the European domestic cat has evolved, and familiar in many a non-pedigree. The tabby markings of a show cat, however, must conform to very exact standards, and most importantly of all, be balanced on both sides of the body. There are three main patterns: the classic tabby, the more markedly striped mackerel, and the spotted. Both have a trio of dark lines running along the spine and distinctive, evenly spaced rings around the neck, tail and legs. The classic, however, has dark spirals of colour on its flanks, a winged shape over the shoulders, and a spotted belly.

Tabby colours range from the thick-cut marmalade variety of red on red, the Brown (the Brown Classic is also described as marbled or blotched) and Silver, to the softer dilutes of Blue and Cream.

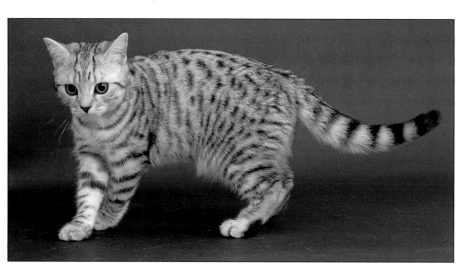

✦ RIGHT
An alert side profile shows the superb mix of colours in a Tortie Silver Tabby, and the shortish but active tail characteristic of the shorthair.

✦ BELOW
The black-on-silver colouring of the Silver Spotted Tabby shows up the tabby markings to dramatic effect, especially the evenly spaced rings on tail and legs.

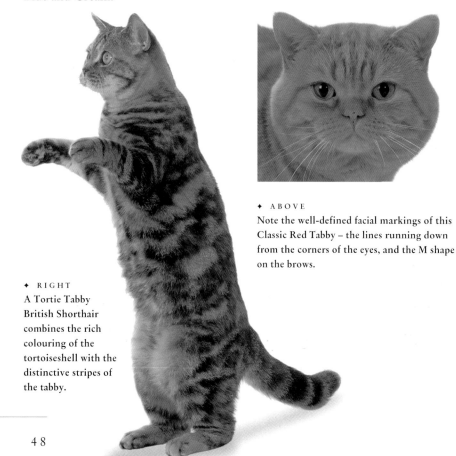

✦ RIGHT
A Tortie Tabby British Shorthair combines the rich colouring of the tortoiseshell with the distinctive stripes of the tabby.

✦ ABOVE
Note the well-defined facial markings of this Classic Red Tabby – the lines running down from the corners of the eyes, and the M shape on the brows.

BREED BOX	
Coat	short, thick, fine
Eyes	round *Classic Tabby:* gold, orange to copper *Silver:* green to hazel
Other features	round-tipped ears; short nose; big round paws; nose leather and paw pads brick-red (and/or black for the Silver Tabby)
Grooming	easy; regular combing
Temperament	companionable, independent, freedom-loving

BRITISH COLOURPOINTED

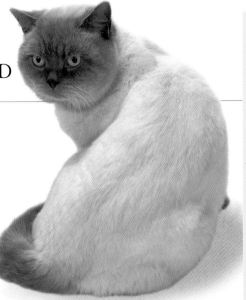

Careful outcrossing of British Shorthairs to Colourpoint Persians resulted in the recent development of the British Shorthair Colourpointed. A certain over-indulgence of hair took a bit of ironing out through breeding programmes, but today's British Shorthair Colourpointed has all the right characteristics of type, with a short, dapper fur coat and sturdy build. The cats come in the same versions of colourpointed as the Siamese, including seal, chocolate, lilac, red and cream. The most recent colours to be accepted are cinnamon and fawn points. All versions have big, round, saucer-like blue eyes, set against the colourpointed mask. The colourpointed features – mask, ears, paws and tail – should be clearly defined in good examples of the breed, and any shading in the body colour should tone in with the point colour.

BREED BOX	
Coat	short, thick, fine
Eyes	round; blue
Other features	round-tipped ears; short nose; big round paws; nose leather and paw pads to tone in with point colour
Grooming	easy; regular combing
Temperament	companionable, independent, freedom-loving

✦ ABOVE LEFT
Classic British build combines with delicate Siamese markings on a British Shorthair Lilac Colourpointed.

BRITISH SHORTHAIR COLOURS AND PATTERNS

Self colours:
White (blue-eyed, orange-eyed, odd-eyed), Black, Chocolate, Lilac, Blue, Cream, Red, Cinnamon and Fawn

Tabby:
Silver, Blue Silver, Chocolate Silver, Lilac Silver, Red Silver, Cream Silver, Black Tortie Silver, Blue-Cream Silver, Chocolate Tortie Silver, Lilac-Cream Silver, Brown, Chocolate, Lilac, Blue, Red, Cream, Brown Tortie, Blue-Cream, Chocolate Tortie and Lilac-Cream
Patterns – classic, mackerel or spotted

Tortoiseshell:
Black Tortie, Chocolate Tortie, Blue-Cream Tortie and Lilac Tortie

Patched:
Black Tortie and White, Blue Tortie and White, Chocolate Tortie and White, Lilac Tortie and White, Black and White, Blue and White, Chocolate and White, Lilac and White, Red and White, Cream and White

Smoke:
All self colours (other than white, cinnamon and fawn) and all the tortoiseshell colours

Tipped:
Sparkling white coat with the very tips of the fur dusted with the self and tortoiseshell colours. The Golden Tipped, the non-silver version, has black tipping

Colourpointed:
Colour restricted to the points which can be in all self, tabby, silver tabby, tortoiseshell and smoke colours. Cats have blue eyes

✦ RIGHT
A line-up of British Shorthair kitten breeds. From left to right, Tortie, Blue, Black, and Cream Spotted. Potential owners must remember that while they retain the sweet nature of the breed, mature Shorthairs are big, heavy cats.

BRITISH TIPPED

Like the Longhaired Persian Chinchilla, the British Tipped Shorthairs have a faint dusting of another colour right at the tips of their predominantly white fur, and at the point of their tails. They also share the classic Chinchilla characteristic of nose and eyes fetchingly outlined in black. The tipping (or chinchillation) – which can be black, blue, red, cream, chocolate, lilac or tortoiseshell colours – is such a mere suggestion that it gives a sense of iridescence when the cat moves. The effect may be concentrated in one or two areas to give a ghost of a patch on the flanks or

◆ RIGHT
Sparkling white dusted with black gives an ethereal shimmer to the coat of this British Black-Tipped Shorthair.

◆ RIGHT
The Golden-tipped British Shorthair is in fact gold with black tipping. This kitten has the well-defined eyes that are characteristic of tipped varieties.

back, or rings on the legs. An outstanding feature of the Black and Golden-tipped British Shorthairs is their brilliant green eye colour. The Golden-tipped, unlike the other British Tipped, has a rich golden-apricot undercoat with black tipping. The tipped colorations developed as a result of complex interbreeding of cats with Silver genes, that determined the undercoat colour, with Blues and Smokes. The non-agouti version of the tipped effect produces the British Smoke, which appears to be a self or plain-coloured cat until the hair is pushed back to see the startling silver undercoat. British Smokes are also bred in the same wide colour range.

BREED BOX	
Coat	short, thick, fine
Eyes	round; copper to gold; green in Black, Golden-tipped
Grooming	light combing
Temperament	companionable, freedom-loving

THE AMERICAN SHORTHAIR

The American Shorthair should, like the British Shorthair, proudly show its ancestry as a working cat in its power-packed body. In fact, it is very similar in appearance to the British version, although rather more lithe with a less rounded face and slightly larger body.

The American Shorthair is the refined, pedigreed version of the domestic cat of America that probably first came over with the pioneering band of Puritans (the Pilgrims) from England in the 1600s. In fact, it was known as the Domestic Shorthair until 1985. It was well suited to the tough life of the men and women who were pushing back the frontiers of a new country – hardy, lithe and an excellent rodent exterminator. As in Europe, its worth as a hunter went hand in hand with an attitude of suspicion and even alarm from the human pioneers.

By the 1700s, however, cats had become established in human family life, and were even included in family portraits. They were also officially accounted for by the United States Post Office. The British artist, author and cat show organizer Harrison Weir recorded in 1889 that the post office cat's job was to protect the mail bags from being eaten by rats and mice. When kittens were born, the postmaster could apply for an increased food ration for them.

Nevertheless, the first Domestic Shorthair (other than Siamese) to be registered as a pedigree cat in the United States was an imported British Shorthair, a Red Tabby. Her owner cross-mated her with a fine American cat, and registered the first Shorthair to be bred in America, a

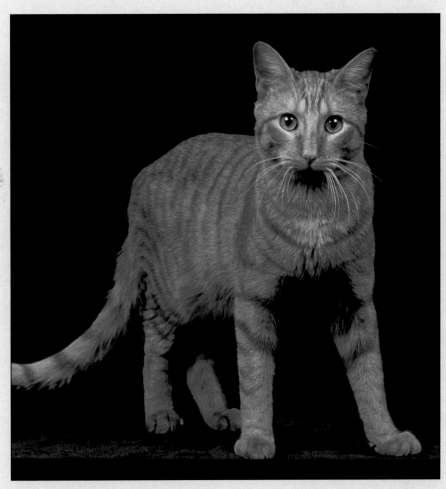

✦ ABOVE
An American Tabby Shorthair shows all the essential lithe muscularity of the breed, well proportioned with neat, well-rounded feet.

Smoke called Buster Brown, in 1904. It took another 60 years for the breed to become an established pedigree in its own right. The most important feature for a show-standard American Shorthair is its strength and muscularity of body. Any sign of weakness in build would penalize it.

The American Cat Fanciers' Association recognizes most of the various solid, shaded, silver, smoke, tabby, parti-colour, bi-colour and van groupings. However, they are resistant to lilac and chocolate self colours and colourpointeds.

BREED BOX

Coat	short, dense, even and firm in texture
Eyes	large, round, wide-set and slightly slanted; brilliant gold, green; white varieties blue-, gold- or odd-eyed
Other features	equable nature and sturdy build
Grooming	easy; regular combing
Temperament	bold, intelligent, inquisitive, active

AMERICAN BLACK SOLID

The perfect example of an American Black Shorthair should have no markings of any colour on its dense black fur, or any sign of rusting. This may mean a limited amount of time in the sunshine for show cats. Nose and paw pads are also black.

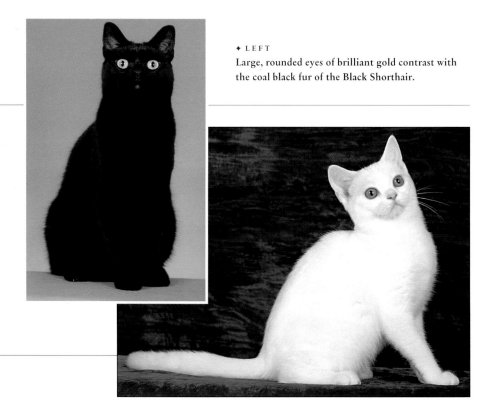

◆ LEFT
Large, rounded eyes of brilliant gold contrast with the coal black fur of the Black Shorthair.

AMERICAN WHITE SOLID

The eyes of the solid white cat may be clear gold, deep blue or even odd-eyed as long as the intensity of each colour is equal. The body should be well-knit and powerful with a full, muscular chest. The variety needs to be pure white with no markings at all.

AMERICAN CREAM

The nose leather and paw pads of an American Cream Shorthair are pink, while the fur is ideally an even buff colour with no markings. Judges tend to prefer light shades. The breed should have sturdy legs.

◆ ABOVE
The sweet expression of this American White Shorthair reflects the amiable and affectionate nature of the breed as a whole.

◆ LEFT
The buttermilk coat of the Cream Shorthair will become thicker in winter months, as with the breed in general.

AMERICAN BI-COLOUR

The Black and White Bi-colour should have a V-shaped blaze on its forehead and upright medium-sized ears, with well-defined patches of black, red, blue or cream on white.

◆ RIGHT
The American Bi-colour's tail is as it should be: thick at the root, rounded at the tip, and medium in length.

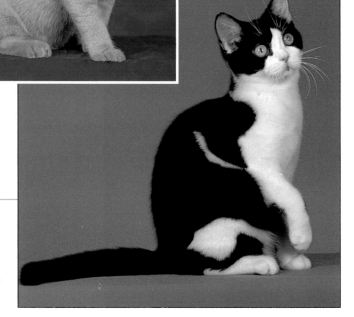

AMERICAN CALICO

This is the classic Calico Cat of America, its pretty coat colour named after a popular printed cotton fabric. This cat shows the preferred predominance of white on the underparts. There are also dilute versions of the colour combination available, in which the white feet, legs, undersides, chest and muzzle are combined with even, unbroken patches of blue and cream.

◆ LEFT
The Calico Cat is also found in a dilute blue and cream version.

◆ BELOW
The coloured patches on an American Tortoiseshell should be scattered over its body.

AMERICAN TORTOISESHELL

An American Tortoiseshell Shorthair typically has a black coat patched with unbroken areas of red and cream. A show-standard cat is required to have well-defined patches distributed over its body. There are various shaded and tipped and tortoiseshell varieties, too, as well as dilute versions. Eyes may be green or bright gold.

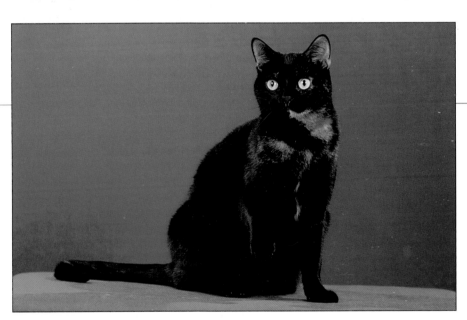

AMERICAN SHADED SILVER

The American Shaded Silver, like the lighter-shaded Chinchilla, ideally has the same level of toning on its face and legs. A distinctive feature of the Shaded and Chinchilla varieties of Shorthair is the black outlining around the eyes and nose.

◆ RIGHT
This Shaded Silver has the rounded head of the breed with well-developed cheeks, and a gently dipping nose.

EUROPEAN SHORTHAIR

The smart version of the feral cat of Europe is a little more streamlined than its British and American counterparts. It is probably the closest of the national shorthairs to the wild species. A clear distinction has been made between British and European Shorthairs since 1982.

The European Shorthair is more elegant than the British, with an emphasis on lithe muscularity rather than round cobbiness. In general shape, it is more like the American Shorthair, though it may be rather larger. It is strong, broad-chested and quite deep in the flank, with fairly long, well-boned legs and rounded paws. The tail is in proportion to the

◆ ABOVE
The leaner features and longer nose of the European Shorthair compared with its British and American equivalents can be seen in this handsome Tabby.

BREED BOX	
Coat	dense; crisp texture
Eyes	slanted, gentle expression; all colours
Other features	territorial, combative towards other cats; prolific breeders
Grooming	easy; regular brushing
Temperament	affectionate, brave, lively, independent; freedom-loving (must not be confined indoors)

body and rounded at the tip, and largish ears are set erect and fairly wide apart.

Unlike the American and British Shorthairs, the European is allowed what is known as open registration in FIFe (the European cat fancy) shows. This means that as long as it conforms to certain standards and characteristic features, and has been assessed and passed by senior judges in Novice classes, any cat may be registered as a foundation pedigree and compete for show titles. Many a worthy European Grand Champion has had its origins in the farmyard! The result of this is that the European Shorthair is particularly adaptable, independent and bright. It also has a remarkably efficient immune system.

◆ LEFT
A pair of European Silver Tabbies display the well-defined "necklaces" and well-spaced leg rings that are characteristic of a good mackerel tabby pattern.

EUROPEAN SHORTHAIR COLOURS AND PATTERNS

Self colours: White (blue-, green- or odd-eyed), Black, Blue, Red, Cream

Tabby: Black, Blue, Red, Cream, Tortie and Blue Tortie
Patterns – classic, mackerel, spotted

Tortoiseshell: Black Tortie, Blue Tortie, Red Tortie

Smoke: Black, Blue, Red, Cream, Tortie and Blue Tortie

Bi-colour, Van, Harlequin: solid colour (Black, Blue, Red, Cream, Tortie, Blue Tortie) plus white

Patched: Black Tortie and White, Blue Tortie and White, Black and White, Blue and White, Red and White, Cream and White

◆ ABOVE
A relatively relaxed attitude to breeding programmes means that there is enormous variety of colour and temperament with the European Shorthair pedigree.

CHARTREUX

The Chartreux is often confused with the British Blue Shorthair, which it closely resembles. There are similarities in robustness, a large, full body, and legs that are shortish in relation to the body. Otherwise, the Chartreux is well-proportioned with large, muscular shoulders, and is rather lighter than its British counterpart,

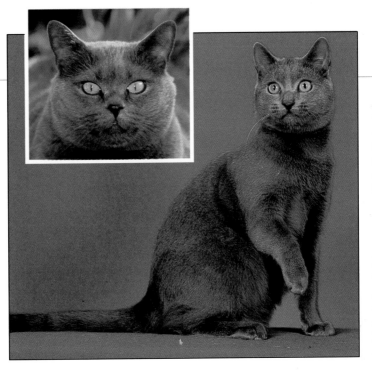

◆ INSET LEFT
A young Chartreux shows off the sweet expression for which the breed is known.

◆ LEFT
The lighter weight of the Chartreux, as compared with the chunkier British Blue Shorthair, is evident in this cat.

BREED BOX

Coat	dense, soft, plush
Eyes	large, round, expressive; pale gold to copper
Other features	large, muscular shoulders; short, strong neck; sweet smiling expression
Grooming	easy; regular brushing
Temperament	calm, affectionate, intelligent

especially in America. Its head is large and broad but not as round as that of the British Shorthair, although the cheeks of adult males are well developed. The nose is short and straight with a slight break, and the muzzle is narrow in relation to the head but not pointed. The Chartreux comes in any shade of blue with silver highlights. It is thought to have been bred in the Middle Ages at the Monastery of La Grande Chartreuse (which was also responsible for the liqueur of the same name). Another version of its origins suggests that the Carthusian order of monks had nothing at all to do with the cat, but that its coat was reminiscent in texture to the fine, wool cloth known as *pile de Chartreux*.

ORIENTAL SHORTHAIR

The ancestors of the Oriental Shorthairs are, like the Siamese, from Thailand. They are, in fact, just like Siamese cats but with all-over coat colour and pattern rather than the Siamese colourpoints on face, ears, tail and legs. The eyes of the Orientals are usually green rather than the blue of the Siamese, although in the solid White, they may be blue or orange (though the British standard rejects the orange-eyed). Virtually all colour and pattern variations are represented, except, of course, the colourpoints, making this one of the most diverse of all cat breeds and groups.

In the United Kingdom and Europe, the self colours were originally known as Foreign Shorthairs but the other varieties have always been

◆ ABOVE
A Red Oriental can show the tabby markings that come with its red genes, but preferably no white hairs at all. You can see this cat's Siamese heritage in its large ears and long, straight nose.

known as Orientals. Each different colour was given a separate breed category to enable the cats to be entered at shows, as they were excluded from the Siamese classes. In the United States in the 1970s, all the variations were grouped together in the one category of Oriental Shorthairs, and this broad term is now universal. However, the British cat fancy still classifies the different colours and patterns as distinct breeds. There are four fundamental sub-divisions: solid colours, shaded, smokes and tabbies.

The Oriental Shorthair type was developed during the 1960s by mating Siamese with indigenous cats such as the British, European and American Shorthairs. They have since only been outcrossed to Siamese, so have a very similar temperament. They enjoy human company generally, and do not like being left alone for too long. In many ways, their response to

◆ ABOVE
The coat of the Havana is a gloriously warm brown. It is a purely Oriental cat, unlike the Havana Brown of the United States.

ORIENTAL COLOURS AND PATTERNS

Foreign White:
White with blue eyes (United Kingdom), or orange or blue eyes (United States)

Self colours:
Chocolate (Havana), Lilac, Black, Blue, Red, Cream, Apricot, Cinnamon, Caramel, Fawn

Tortoiseshell:
as self colours

Oriental Smoke:
any colour with a near-white undercoat

Oriental Shaded:
shaded or tipped with any colour with or without silver

Oriental Tabbies:
spotted, classic or mackerel pattern in all colours with or without silver

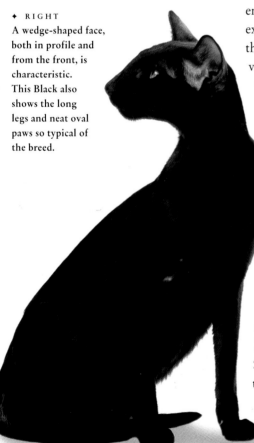

◆ RIGHT
A wedge-shaped face, both in profile and from the front, is characteristic. This Black also shows the long legs and neat oval paws so typical of the breed.

BREED BOX

Coat	short, soft, fine, lying flat along the body
Eyes	almond-shaped, slanted; green with no flecks (except Foreign White – brilliant blue)
Other features	loud voice as in Siamese, large ears, big personality
Grooming	easy; can be "polished" with a soft glove
Temperament	intelligent, lively, inquisitive, active, need company

✦ ABOVE
Apart from a wide range of self colours, the Oriental Shorthair comes in every shade and pattern of tabby. This Chocolate Classic Tabby may have a Siamese and a good quality, but non-pedigreed, Tabby in its distant ancestry.

✦ BELOW
This black-on-silver Spotted Tabby was once known in the United Kingdom as the Egyptian Mau. Now it is classified as an Oriental Shorthair, and the Mau is quite a different breed.

humans is dog-like – they may run to greet their owners on their return home, and need to be played with. Their athletic physique has also led to canine comparisons – their length of body and the way they move is like the feline version of a whippet, complete with whip-like tail.

✦ ABOVE
A Spotted Tabby demonstrates that the back legs of the Oriental Shorthair are longer than its forelegs, and that the general body line suggests slender strength.

SIAMESE

The distinctive masked features, dark paws and tail of the Seal Point Siamese cat were described in a 15th-century manuscript of cat poems discovered in Siam (modern Thailand) – which suggests that the cats were already deeply established in the national consciousness. The Seal Point became the Royal Cat of Siam. It could only be obtained from the royal palace in Bangkok by special favour of the King. When members of the royal family died, the cats were thought to aid transmigration of their souls. A cat was placed in the tomb with the deceased. Evidence of its escape through holes in the ceiling of the chamber confirmed that the soul had successfully travelled to the afterlife.

The first breeding pair of Siamese reached Britain in 1884. The required standards then – for what are known as Traditional Siamese (also known as Apple Heads, Opals or Thai Siamese) – called for much stockier cats, rounder in the head than later lines. Their ears were quite small, and their coats as dense and plushy as moleskin. The cats also had a pronounced squint and a kink in the end of their tails, typical of the genetic inheritance of cats throughout south-east Asia, and which are considered defects in the modern pedigree. The Traditional Siamese is still popular among those people who seek a cat less extreme in type than those approved of today by show judges.

The modern Siamese is long-bodied and long-limbed with dainty oval paws. Face on, its head from the tip of the large, triangular ears to the muzzle is a pronounced wedge shape.

SEAL POINT

The original Siamese cat, as described in a 15th-century Thai manuscript, was clearly already well-known at that time. The coat is fawn and the points darken to almost black on the nose and ears. The strong contrast in colour between the points and the pale, even cream of the main area of the coat is important. The dark brown seal points should be restricted to a triangle on the face, the ears, legs and tail. Nose and paw pads are matching dark brown.

◆ ABOVE
Illustrations of a cat with dark points like this modern Seal Point Siamese have been found in a centuries-old manuscript from Thailand.

◆ LEFT
A Seal Point shows off the perfectly balanced lines of the pedigree Siamese, with long neck, long legs and long body following through to the tip of the tail.

CHOCOLATE POINT

Some Seal Points were naturally lighter than others. This characteristic was eventually developed into the Chocolate Point. The brown extremities are a milk-chocolate brown rather than the rich plain chocolate of the Seal Point. The body colour is ivory.

◆ RIGHT
An alert and enquiring mind is suggested by the attitude of this American Chocolate Point.

BREED BOX (ALL VARIATIONS)	
Coat	very short, fine, glossy and close-lying
Eyes	almond-shaped, slanted; alert, intelligent expression; clear brilliant blue
Other features	loud voice, large ears, big personality
Grooming	easy; must be done regularly
Temperament	intelligent, lively, playful, loyal, affectionate but can be aloof

BLUE POINT

The essence of the Blue Point is a main body colour of icy white with mere hints of the pale bluish-brown of the points. The Blue was one of the early variations of the breed to gain acceptance. It is a dilute form of the Seal.

◆ LEFT
The long, straight Roman nose and startling blue eye colour of the breed are finely demonstrated by this Blue Point.

LILAC (FROST) POINT

As its alternative American name suggests, a main body colour with just a hint of off-white moves into the frosted blue-grey of the points. There is a touch of lavender in the point colour, meeting its match in complementary lavender-pink nose and paw pads. This is the dilute form of the Chocolate.

◆ RIGHT
A Lilac Point is carrying on a conversation even while it is being photographed. Siamese are the most vocal and extrovert of cats.

59

RED POINT

The introduction of the sex-linked orange gene contributed to the Red Point. The points should be reddish-gold with pink nose leather and paw pads, all set off against an ivory coat.

◆ RIGHT
In a Red Point Siamese, the deeper and more intense the eye colour the better – it makes a dramatic contrast against the red-gold points.

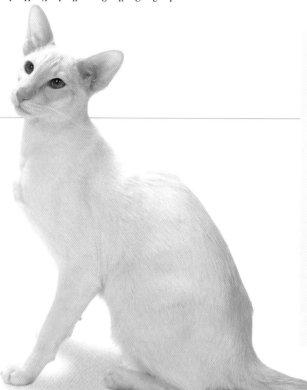

SIAMESE COLOUR GROUPS

United Kingdom:
Seal, Blue, Chocolate, Lilac, Red, Cream, Cinnamon, Fawn, Caramel and Apricot with their Tabby and Tortie combinations

United States:
Only Seal, Blue, Chocolate and Lilac are recognized. All other colour combinations are available but are grouped in the category of Colourpointed Shorthairs

In some Federations and Associations worldwide, the Siamese is also recognized with Silver-based points, e.g. the Seal Smoke Point

CREAM POINT

Cream on cream brings an extremely subtle tonal difference. The slightly richer buttermilk points are barely discernible against an ivory coat. Nose and paw pads are pink. The Cream Point is a dilute version of the Red.

◆ BELOW
The fur of a Cream Point Siamese shows dense cream points and the palest of cream bodies, against which the eyes are a deep sapphire blue.

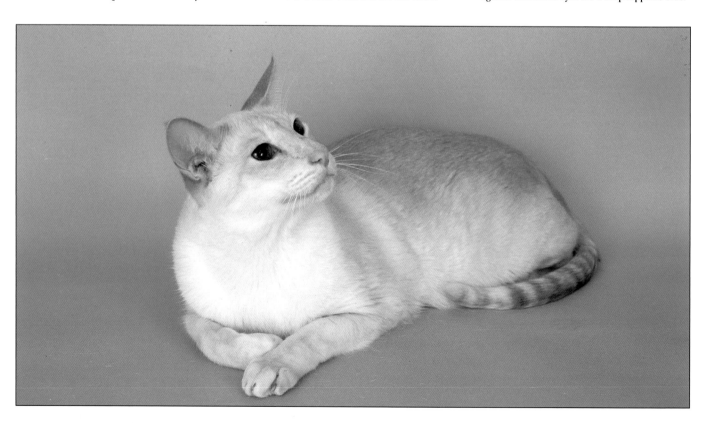

TABBY POINT (LYNX POINT)

There are now many variations of Tabby-pointed Siamese. In the United States only the traditional Seal, Blue, Chocolate and Lilac pointed varieties are recognized, so the Tabby joins all other variations under the category of Colourpointed Shorthairs.

In the United Kingdom, Tabby and Tortoiseshell variations are accepted, even in the new colours such as Fawn, Cinnamon and Caramel.

◆ ABOVE RIGHT
This is a Chocolate Tabby Point, showing clearly defined rings on the tail, and a lovely pale, creamy main body colour to contrast with the points.

PATCHED ORIENTALS

Yet another group linked with the Siamese are the Patched Orientals. These are in essence white Siamese cats with distinct patches of colour or tortoiseshell. Such bi-colour and tortoiseshell and white combinations were previously seen before only in Persians and British Shorthairs. Siamese were mated to patched Cornish Rex cats. Constant back-crossing to Siamese and appropriate Orientals slowly eliminated the Cornish Rex type and increased the amount of white, so that the required balance of white to colour was achieved. These are not recognized by the British cat fancy or by many overseas organizations.

TORTIE POINT

In the United States, the Tortie Point Siamese is bracketed under the more general Colourpointed classification. In the United Kingdom, there are very specific standards. The main requirement is that, as with any of the Siamese, the points are in contrast to the body colour. They should be randomly mottled with various shades of red and cream on whatever the base colour might be. There are Tortie Points in the newer colours, such as Cinnamon, as well as the traditional Seal, Blue and Chocolate.

◆ RIGHT
A lactating Chocolate Tortie Point queen has all the essential Siamese type characteristics, including a tendency to thrash its tail when bored with the photo session!

SNOWSHOE

Rounded, snow-white paws are a most distinct feature of this cat. The Snowshoe is also a unique combination of the Himalayan, or Siamese point pattern, with white spotting. It was

◆ LEFT
The ideal standard recommended for the Snowshoe includes an inverted V between the eyes, which this Blue Point does not quite achieve.

BREED BOX	
Coat	medium short, glossy, close-lying
Eyes	large, almond-shaped; bright, sparkling blue
Other features	white paws
Grooming	easy; regular, gentle brushing
Temperament	Siamese bounce with American Shorthair placidity

the occasional tendency of Siamese cats to have white feet (which was long perceived as a fault) that inspired the Snowshoe's American breeder into action in the 1960s. The Snowshoe inherited its white spotting, and its bulk, from the American Shorthair. However, the long body, point colour, and bounce in its personality come from its Oriental background.

It is a well-balanced and very muscular cat, and when the white is symmetrically marked against the dark points, can be most striking.

The front feet are ideally white only as far as the ankles, while there is a longer gauntlet to the hock on the back legs. The Snowshoe, sometimes known as Silver Laces, is recognized in Seal Point and Blue Point colours.

SEYCHELLOIS

The Seychellois is another example of an attempt to create a new, oriental-type breed. It is a cross between a Tortie and White Persian and Siamese. The long coat of the Persian has not been entirely lost and the variety is recognized (as "unrecognized colour") by the British Cat Association in both

◆ RIGHT
A chocolate and white Seychellois shows its Siamese origins in the distinctive point colours.

BREED BOX	
Coat	very short, fine, glossy; also semi-longhair variety
Eyes	blue
Grooming	easy

coat lengths. It is fundamentally a cat of slender oriental build and features, with a white coat splashed with various colours. There are three variations,

according to the proportion of white in relation to coloured areas: Septième (Seventh), Huitième (Eighth) and Neuvième (Ninth). All have blue eyes.

ABYSSINIAN

Today's pedigree Abyssinian looks like the sacred cats that are depicted in ancient Egyptian tomb paintings. The name comes from the country to the south-east of Egypt that is known as Ethiopia today. The modern Abyssinian is essentially a ticked tabby cat, with tabby markings reduced to a minimum by many years of selective breeding. Some theories suggest that the cat was introduced to the West by

♦ RIGHT
The Fawn Abyssinian is one of the newer colours that has been developed in the United Kingdom.

British soldiers returning from the region in the 1860s. Another claims the breed has its origins in the small African wild cat *Felis libyca*, an example of which was found in Abyssinia and presented to a Dutch natural history museum between 1833 and 1882. The breed was, in any event, established enough to be exhibited at the early cat shows of the 1800s.

Hybridization with domestic cats displaying the ticked tabby pattern gradually diluted the exotic blood. A typical ticked tabby has prominent tabby markings on the head, chest, legs and tail, but in the modern Abyssinian, these have been diluted by breeding ticked tabby to ticked tabby. Residual tabby markings may occur around the eyes, as a dark line along the spine to the tip of the tail, or as faint broken necklets and leg bars. The Abyssinian is a medium-sized, lithe and muscular cat with an arching, elegant neck. Large, cupped ears are set wide apart. The Wild Abyssinian attempts to recreate

the look of the early Abyssinian cat when it first came to Europe, but is not yet a recognized breed with any reputable organization. It retains the reduced ticked tabby pattern but has a slightly larger conformation than the usual varieties.

BREED BOX

Coat	short, close-lying, fine but not soft; distinctly ticked, resulting in at least four bands of colour – the roots of the fur are the colour of the base hair, and the final band is ticking colour
Eyes	wide set, large, expressive, slanting, almond shaped; amber, hazel or green
Grooming	easy
Temperament	intelligent, inquisitive, very energetic, playful, loyal; freedom-loving and enjoy hunting

USUAL (RUDDY)

The original, or Usual, Abyssinian equates to the brown tabby coat colours. The rich golden brown base colour is ticked with black. The nose leather is brick red and the paw pads are black. In America the colour is known as Ruddy, and is one of the four colours recognized there. The others are Red (the British Sorrel), Blue, and Fawn.

♦ RIGHT
The Usual (Ruddy) Abyssinian coat is sable-like with short fur. All Abyssinian coats share the ticked characteristic, in which each hair is banded with two or three colours. In this case, reddish-brown is topped with darker brown and/or black.

SORREL (RED)

The Sorrel Abyssinian, which was the second colour to be recognized in the modern era, was originally known – and is still known in America – as the Red because of the warm, gingery colour of its coat. The bright apricot base coat is ticked with dark brown. Nose leather and paw pads are pink.

ABYSSINIAN COLOURS AND PATTERNS	
Usual (Ruddy), Blue, Sorrel (Red), Fawn, Chocolate, Lilac, Red, Cream	
Silver	in all above colour variations
Tortoiseshell	Usual, Blue, Fawn, Chocolate and Lilac, and Silver versions of these

✦ RIGHT
The handsome, muscular physique of the Sorrel is typical of the breed. Abyssinians are lithe enough, but slightly bulkier than Oriental Shorthairs, and their heads are more rounded.

FAWN

The Fawn Abyssinian is a fairly recent addition to the plain colour range. It has a pale-oatmeal base coat powdered with darker, warm brown ticking. The fur pales to cream at the tips of tail and ears, on the toe tufts and at the back of the paws. Nose leather and paw pads are pink.

✦ BELOW
The long bodyline balanced by a firm tail and the slender but powerful legs of this Fawn Abyssinian are typical of the breed as a whole.

BLUE

✦ BELOW
The demeanour of this Blue, with its lynx-like ears and feral look to the eyes, lends credence to the possibility that Abyssinians may be the wild ancestors of the European domestic cat.

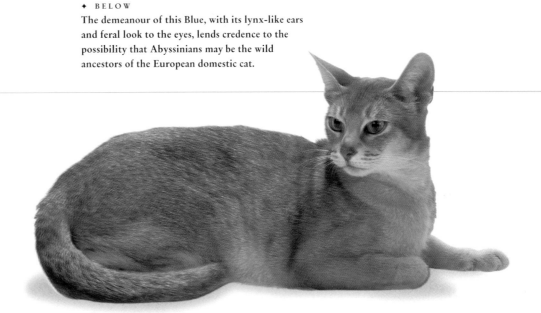

Blue Abyssinian kittens occasionally occur in the litters of Usual-coloured parents. This is due to two recessive genes of the type that trigger the dilution pairing up and therefore being able to "come out" or be expressed. The undercoat is pinkish-beige ticked with slate grey. Nose leather and paw pads are dark pink to mauve-blue.

LILAC

The undercoat of the Lilac variety is pinkish-cream ticked with a slightly deeper hue of soft pinkish-grey. The nose leather and paw pads are mauve-pink, and eyes, as with all Abyssinians, range from amber to hazel or green.

✦ RIGHT
A Lilac kitten has a distinct break in the line of its nose, and has the expressive eyes and pricked ears desirable of the breed.

SILVER

The Silver Abyssinian is recognized as an official breed in the United Kingdom and Europe, but not in the United States. The colour variations are Sorrel, Blue, Chocolate, Lilac, Fawn, Red and Cream. All have pinkish to mauve nose leather and paw pads, apart from the Usual, which has a brick-red nose and black paw pads. All variations have a silver base coat ticked with the appropriate colour.

✦ RIGHT
One way of judging whether this Silver's tail is long enough for the required pedigree standard is to estimate whether it would reach the cat's shoulders if laid along the back.

RUSSIAN BLUE

◆ LEFT
A Russian Blue gives an impression of making a complaint, but in fact its voice is so quiet that it is sometimes not even obvious when the queens are calling.

As befits a cat that is said to originate from the fringe of the Arctic Circle (and have a possible Norwegian connection, too), the most distinctive feature of today's Russian Blue is its double overcoat.

From the very start of the cat fancy, two types of Blue cat came into competition with each other at shows all over the world. The domestic British Shorthair was one; the other was known as the Blue Foreign. The names suggest a distinct difference in type between the two varieties.

Blue cats were reputed to have reached the West via merchant ships travelling from the port of Archangel in northern Russia, and became known as Archangel cats. Another import was a blue tabby from Norway. There were probably several other blues from other parts of the world that may have

◆ ABOVE
The Russian Blue has pronounced whisker pads, wide-set, pointed ears and a face more rounded than that of other foreign shorthairs. These combine to give the cat a gentle expression that reflects its nature.

◆ RIGHT
Top-quality coat texture is the single most important point that judges look for in a Russian Blue. It should be dense beneath and fine and short on top.

helped the true blue breeding programme. The type is also known as the Maltese Blue and the Spanish Blue. By the late 1800s, there were enough Blues bred to be shown at the early cat shows. Unlike the cats of today, though, these early Blues had orange eyes.

Later breeding programmes included the Korat and British Blue Shorthairs. Just before and after World War II, a bid to save the Blue from extinction led to the inclusion of a Blue Point Siamese in one breeding programme, and until fairly recently the occasional Siamese pattern was subsequently found in litters of Russian Blues. Siamese characteristics are now regarded as unacceptable in the breed.

Imports of Blues were brought in from Scandinavia, and many good Russians went to the United States where the standard colour is a little lighter than that required in Europe.

There must be no hint of white or tabby markings on the perfect Russian Blue, but there is a silver sheen to its coat, as the slate-blue hairs often have transparent tips. A medium-sized cat, it combines sturdiness with grace. A gentle expression reflects its reputation as a quiet-spoken, affectionate animal.

An English breeder of Russian Blues maintained that the Russian type referred to a particular shape rather than the colour. Using a white, double-coated female found near the London docks, she began to develop Russian cats in other colours. The project appears to have died out in Britain, but there is a thriving colony of coloured cats in the Netherlands.

BREED BOX	
Coat	plush, heavy, double; brush-like from the body
Eyes	almond-shaped; green
Other features	silver sheen to coat as hairs often have transparent tips
Grooming	easy; gentle, regular brushing so as not to damage the double coat texture
Temperament	quiet, gentle, affectionate

KORAT

In Thailand, a wedding gift of a pair of Korats brings good fortune and happiness. There is no doubt that the Korat has been known for several hundred years. It is one of the distinctive Thai cats (alongside the Siamese and Burmese) described and illustrated in the 16th-century (or earlier) *Cat-Book of Poems* manuscript

◆ ABOVE
The Korat's heart-shaped face is typical; so is the luminous green of its eyes, and the way in which they are round and prominent when open, but appear slanted when closed.

BREED BOX

Coat	short to medium length; thick, silky; no undercoat
Eyes	round, large, luminous, prominent; green – colour changes during the course of the cat's early years
Other features	quietly vocal
Grooming	easy; regular brushing and combing
Temperament	loving, very playful

◆ LEFT
A distinctive feature of the Korat is its coat. It shows a subtle silvery tipping.

in the national library in Bangkok. A verse on the Korat reads:

The hairs are smooth with roots like clouds and tips like silver. The eyes shine like dewdrops on a lotus leaf.

It is not surprising that the Korats captured the attention of American soldiers serving in Thailand, and the first was imported into the United States in 1959 (they reached Britain in 1972). The breed attained championship status in America in 1966. The Korat Cat Fanciers' Association was founded in 1965 with the declaration: "The Korat is silver-blue from birth to death. It can exist in no other colour. If any other colour should occur it would automatically cease to be a Korat." Nevertheless, it

appeared that the original imports were not as pure as originally thought, and that a recessive dilute gene might result in the occasional lilac, blue point or lilac point kitten. These have been named as the Thai Lilac and Thai Pointed variations.

The Korat is a medium-sized, lithe and muscular cat, and the females are daintier than the males. The most distinguishing features are the large green eyes set in a heart-shaped face and the silvery sheen of the coat.

◆ RIGHT
The Thai Lilac reflects recessive genetic traits found in the Blue Korat.

BURMESE

Brown, stocky, smooth-haired cats very like the modern pedigreed Burmese are illustrated in a 16th-century (or earlier) Thai manuscript called the *Cat-Book of Poems*. They are described in the manuscript as *supalak* (copper) cats. Early in the 1900s, a small brown cat was taken from Burma to England and described as a Chocolate Siamese. However, it was not approved of in competition with the Seal Point Siamese, and nothing became of it as a breed.

The foundation of today's Burmese line was eventually laid in the early 1930s. A small brown female of Burmese origin, but probably a hybrid similar to today's Tonkinese, was mated with a Seal Point Siamese in San Francisco. Some of the resulting offspring were dark brown and formed the beginnings of the official pedigree Burmese. The breed was registered by the American Cat Fanciers' Federation in 1936, and in the late 1940s gained rapid acceptance in the United Kingdom. Despite having a genetic pattern almost identical to the Siamese, the Burmese is quieter-voiced, and much more compact of build. Its nose is distinctly different too, having an obvious bend, or break, in its line. The breed is particularly known for having a delightful personality, being sunny of temperament and obviously intelligent. The cats have well-proportioned legs, with the back legs slightly shorter than the front, and neat, oval paws. The tail is straight and of medium length, tapering to a rounded tip.

BREED BOX	
Coat	short, fine, glossy, satiny, close-lying
Eyes	wide-set, large, round; yellow to gold
Grooming	little extra grooming is necessary
Temperament	intelligent, active, inquisitive, adaptable, friendly

BROWN (SABLE)

The Brown Burmese is the Usual or original colour, and should be warm and rich in tone with matching brown nose leather and paw pads. (The Chocolate, or Champagne, which was introduced later, is more of a milk-chocolate colour.) Some kittens have faint markings but these usually disappear as they mature. As with all the solid colours of Burmese, the fur lightens in shade on the underparts. Similarly, darker areas may be evident on the ears, mask and tail, like ghosts of the seal points of a Siamese.

♦ RIGHT
The top line of the Burmese's eye slants towards the nose, while the lower line is distinctly rounded, giving the breed its unique expression.

♦ RIGHT
A Brown Burmese shows the breed's tendency to rotundity – unlike its compatriots, the lithe Siamese.

BLUE

The first Blue Burmese was sired in the United Kingdom by an imported American cat. It was the Burmese equivalent of its genetic cousin, the Blue Point

Siamese. The ideal tone is soft, silvery slate-blue, with the silver effect more pronounced on ears, cheeks and paws. Nose leather is dark grey and paw pads are a lighter, pinkish-grey.

✦ RIGHT AND LEFT
The density of a Blue Burmese's fur accentuates strong shoulders and a broad, rounded chest. The Burmese is quite a heavy cat for its size!

LILAC (PLATINUM) AND CHOCOLATE

Lilac – or Platinum as it is called in the United States – is a dilute version of the Chocolate (Champagne) Burmese. It became established in the early

1970s. It is a wonderfully soft shade of pinkish dove-grey, and nose leather and paw pads are lavender-pink in keeping.

✦ LEFT
The typical Burmese head is distinctly round, with a short nose and a firm chin, and round-tipped ears spaced well apart. This Lilac shows excellent type.

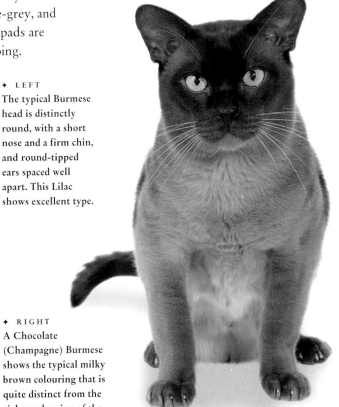

✦ RIGHT
A Chocolate (Champagne) Burmese shows the typical milky brown colouring that is quite distinct from the richer colouring of the Brown (Sable).

RED

The ideal Red has golden eyes and a tangerine-cream colour to its fur, rather than red. Although tabby markings are almost inevitable on the face because of the orange gene which reveals the tabby pattern, the rest of the coat should be consistent in tone. Any hint of rings on the legs would be considered a fault by show judges. Nose leather and paw pads are pink.

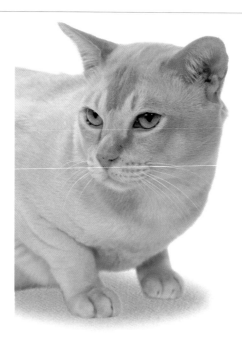

◆ RIGHT
You can see the marked kink in the nose of this Red Burmese. This is known as a nose break and is a feature of the breed in general.

BURMESE COLOURS AND PATTERNS

Solid colours	Brown (Sable), Blue, Chocolate (Champagne), Lilac (Platinum), Red, Cream
Tortoiseshell	Brown, Blue, Chocolate, Lilac

Note that while these varieties are those that are available, not all are recognized as Burmese by every national cat registering body. In the United States, colours outside Sable, Blue, Champagne and Platinum are grouped by the CFA as Foreign Burmese. Other associations call them Malayan.

CREAM

The Cream Burmese was first developed in the United Kingdom in the late 1960s and early 1970s. It is part of the group of colours that arise from the sex-linked orange gene. A Cream Burmese is the dilute version of the Red. If the eyes of a Cream Burmese are deep gold rather than yellow, that is a bonus for the show cat. Otherwise, the ideal coat colour is for an even shade of rich cream moving to slightly darker shades on the ears, face, paws and tail. Paw pads and nose leather are pink.

◆ LEFT
Basic cream is mingled with pinkish dove grey in the Lilac Tortie. There are also Brown, Blue and Chocolate Torties.

◆ RIGHT
Powderings of colour over mask, paws, tail and legs on the Cream Burmese are like ghostly versions of the points on a Siamese.

THE ASIAN GROUP

The Asian Group of cats are Burmese in type, but not in colour, coat pattern or (in the case of the Tiffanie) length of fur. It is a similar relationship to the one between the Siamese and the similar type, but differently coloured and patterned, Oriental Shorthairs, Balinese and Angora. The Asian Group embraces the Asian Self, including the Bombay, the Burmilla and the tabby varieties. The semi-longhaired version of the Asian is the Tiffanie, described in the Semi-longhair section. As with the Burmese, the female Asians are markedly smaller and daintier than the males, but the body type is generally medium-sized, straight-backed and rounded of chest. Legs are medium length with oval paws, and the hind legs are a little longer than the forelegs. The Asian cats carry their medium to long tails high and proud, and the glossiness of their short, close-lying coats is an accurate reflection of their good health.

BREED BOX	
Coat	short, dense, soft and glossy; slightly longer than Burmese
Eyes	yellow to green, green preferred in Silvers, gold allowed in Selfs
Other features	outlined eyes, nose and lips
Grooming	little extra grooming needed
Temperament	stable, dignified inquisitive, sociable

BURMILLA

The Burmilla is the longest established and most popular of the Asian Group of cats, and often the starting point for breeding other varieties. It was the originator of the Asian Group of cats in the United Kingdom, derived from a Lilac Burmese queen and a Chinchilla Silver Persian in 1981. The result was a shorthaired Burmese lookalike with the stunning tipping and outlined features of the Chinchilla. The Burmilla is the shaded or tipped representative of the Asian Group. The shaded varieties are more heavily tipped and obviously coloured than the tipped varieties. The undercoat on both variations is the palest possible silver or golden, but tipped at the very ends with one of the standard or Burmese colours. Nose leather and paw pads are brick-red (terracotta), and dark

◆ LEFT
A Brown-shaded Silver Burmilla expresses the typical inquisitive nature of its type.

◆ RIGHT
On the forehead of the Burmilla there should be an M-shaped mark – as on this Blue Shaded. Other painted face features may be streaks from the outer edges of the eyes and on the cheeks.

◆ ABOVE
The Lilac Tortie Burmilla has a white base coat shaded with a mingling of frosted pink-grey, and dark and light cream. Nose leather and paw pads are complementary lavender or pink; eyes are either amber or green.

BURMILLA COLOURS AND PATTERNS

Standard	gold base coat
Silver	white base coat; colours less intense

May be shaded or tipped with Black, Blue, Chocolate, Lilac, Red, Caramel, Apricot, Cream, Black Tortoiseshell, Blue Tortoiseshell, Chocolate Tortoiseshell, Lilac Tortoiseshell, Caramel Tortoiseshell, plus the Burmese versions of these colours

pigmentation around the eyes, nose and lips should be obvious. One of the cat's particularly appealing features is the outlining of nose and eyes in the same colour as the darker tip. The Burmilla consolidates many of the best points of its parents. It is open and sociable like the Burmese but less demanding and noisy; it is stable and dignified like its Persian forebears, but is rather more adventurous and inquisitive.

♦ ABOVE LEFT
A Black Shaded Silver Burmilla is closest in colour to its Chinchilla Silver heritage and has Chinchilla-like kohl-ringed eyes.

♦ BELOW
Subtle gradations of tone are a delightful feature of the Asian Smoke. This is a Brown, with darker points on tail and face, due to a Burmese gene.

ASIAN SMOKE

The Asian Smoke is, as its name suggests, the smoke variety of the Asian Group. Each hair is silver, while the tip is coloured. Mere suggestions of tabby markings may appear like watered silk on the body, while the head has what are sometimes known as clown marks – frown lines on the forehead and spectacled eyes.

ASIAN SMOKE COLOURS AND PATTERNS

Black, Blue, Chocolate, Lilac, Red, Caramel, Apricot, Cream, Black Tortoiseshell, Blue Tortoiseshell, Chocolate Tortoiseshell, Lilac Tortoiseshell, Caramel Tortoiseshell, plus the Burmese versions of all these colours, all with a silvery-white undercoat

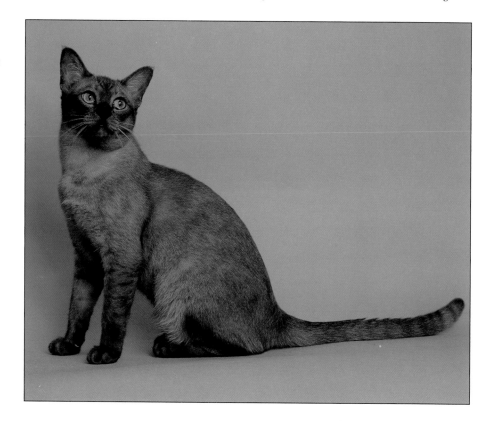

BOMBAY

Because there is an Indian black leopard as sleek and black of coat as this particular domestic cat breed, the Bombay cat is named after an Indian city. The cat's most outstanding features are its gleaming black fur and its large, brilliant golden eyes.

The Bombay was created in the United States in the 1950s in an attempt to breed a pure black Burmese. A Sable (Brown) Burmese was crossed with a Black American Shorthair, and the Bombay was accepted as a championship variety in 1976. An American couple, fittingly named Opium and Bagheera, were exported to France in 1989 to found the European line, and so the type is similar on both sides of the Atlantic.

Not so in the United Kingdom, where Black British Shorthairs were mated with Burmese (although one was later combined with an American Bombay) and ultimately became part of the Asian Group breeding programme. The Bombay is judged in the United Kingdom along the same lines as other Asian self colours. The Bombay on both

♦ ABOVE
With a solid, jet-black coat and deep amber eyes, the Bombay earned the nickname "the patent leathered kid with the new penny eyes" in America, its country of origin.

BREED BOX	
Coat	short, very close-lying and shiny
Eyes	large; gold, yellow to green (United Kingdom); gold to copper (United States)
Other features	patent leather glossiness of coat
Grooming	little extra grooming is necessary
Temperament	sedate, affectionate, needs attention

sides of the Atlantic has a distinct Burmese temperament, is known to purr a great deal, and is a strong and healthy breed. It is a medium-sized cat with a round head that seems large for its body. It has a short snub nose, firm chin and large ears rounded at the tips. Everything about it is black, from the fur that must be jet-black to the tips, to the nose and paw pads.

♦ ABOVE
The Bombay is a polished, all-black Burmese type.

♦ LEFT
Although the black Bombay is the best known self-coloured Asian, there are many other colours. This Blue had black parents somewhere along the line, each of whom carried a recessive gene that resulted in its dilute colour.

OTHER ASIANS

Once the Chinchilla/Lilac Burmese combination had launched the Asian Group, it became evident that an enormous number of variations could occur. Parents were introduced into breeding programmes that carried the sex-linked red gene to produce red, cream, apricot and tortoiseshell Asians. The tabby genes were included for ticked, classic, mackerel and spotted patterns. Colours allowed are Black (Brown), Blue, Chocolate, Lilac, Red, Cream, Caramel and Apricot, all with Silver and their appropriate tortoiseshell combinations, plus the Burmese versions of these colours.

✦ LEFT
The Asian Black Ticked Tabby is more heavily ticked than the Burmilla equivalent. The darkest fur is along the line of the spine, shading to a much paler colour on the underparts and legs.

BREED BOX

Coat	fine, glossy, silky
Eyes	wide-set, large, round; colour ranges from yellow to green; self colours may be golden
Grooming	little extra grooming is necessary
Temperament	easygoing, playful, gentle

ASIAN GROUP COLOURS AND PATTERNS

Self colours	Black (Bombay), Blue, Chocolate, Lilac, Red, Cream, Caramel, Apricot
Tortoiseshell	Black, Blue, Chocolate, Lilac, Caramel
Tabby	classic, spotted, mackerel and ticked patterns in all the above colours and the Burmese versions of these colours, in both Standard and Silver tabby.

✦ ABOVE
Although it has a fine M on its forehead, this is not a tabby, but a Red Self Asian. It is similar to the Red Burmese, but of a considerably deeper, richer and more solid hue.

✦ BELOW
The Caramel Ticked Tabby is one of the rarer dilute colours seen in the Asian Group. This youngster has an excellent M mark on its forehead which will win it a few points.

✦ LEFT
The dominant Tortie colour is black, which this Asian shows very well. The colours can be mingled or in blotches as long as the hairs are coloured to the roots.

BENGAL

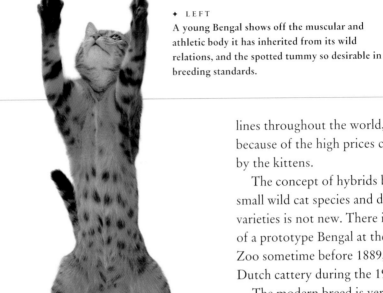

◆ LEFT
A young Bengal shows off the muscular and athletic body it has inherited from its wild relations, and the spotted tummy so desirable in breeding standards.

The Bengal was developed in an attempt to combine the look of the wild Asian Leopard Cat with the temperament of the domesticated cat. Because this involved crossing domestic cats with the wild cats indigenous to south-east Asia, the breeding programmes have met with some controversy. To gain acceptance, it needs to establish that wild tendencies have been bred out, and that the new breed has the ability to reproduce a consistent type. The first Bengal litters born of wild/domestic parents (known as the F1 generation) tended to produce non-fertile males and only partially fertile females, and in some cases the temperament has been unstable. Most associations, therefore, do not allow these early generations to be shown, and they are often not suitable as pets.

Although the modern breed was pioneered in the desert state of Arizona in the United States during the 1960s, it is not registered as a championship breed by all American cat associations. Most of the American varieties are shades of brown. The Bengal is on its way to gaining provisional status in the United Kingdom, where spotted and marbled variations are being bred. There has been a huge increase in Bengal breeding lines throughout the world, possibly because of the high prices commanded by the kittens.

The concept of hybrids between small wild cat species and domestic varieties is not new. There is a record of a prototype Bengal at the London Zoo sometime before 1889, and at a Dutch cattery during the 1960s.

The modern breed is very striking: it is long, sleek and muscular with beautifully patterned fur. Its coat is its unique feature, quite unlike any other domestic breed, being more akin to the feel of a wild cat's pelt. Smallish, forward-pointing ears extend straight up from the sides of the broadly wedge-shaped head.

◆ ABOVE
This Leopard Spotted youngster is beginning to show the desirable patterns that will be clearly outlined in maturity, but at present are slightly masked by the woolly kitten coat.

◆ ABOVE
The Snow Spotted Bengal is a paler version of the spotted variety. The pale background colour is the result of the recessive Siamese gene, and is complemented by clear blue eyes.

◆ LEFT
A Marbled Bengal displays the dramatic coat pattern and long, prowling bodyline.

BREED BOX	
Coat	short to medium, very dense; and unusually soft to the touch
Eyes	oval, large, not bold
Grooming	regular stroking; some brushing
Temperament	active, playful, loves water

TONKINESE

For those who regard the modern Siamese as rather rat-like in its sleekness, and the American Burmese as too Persian and heavyweight, the Tonkinese is, perhaps, a compromise. The breed is also seen as having the points of the Siamese but with a more softly contoured body and a less assertive nature.

The Tonk is the product of mating Siamese and Burmese in America during the 1950s and the following two decades, although the type had occurred spontaneously for a long time. Such mixed parentage means no all-Tonk litters. The offspring from a Tonkinese coupling is likely to be two Tonks, one Siamese, and one Burmese. The Tonkinese cat type displays the mingled characteristics of the two breeds – of medium build, it has a gently wedge-shaped head rounded at the top, though slightly longer than

that of the Siamese. Like the Burmese, there is an angle on its shortish nose, but it is not as pronounced. Tonkinese legs are slim but muscular, and its body is a perfect balance between the length of the Siamese and the

✦ ABOVE
Originally the result of a cross mating between Burmese and Siamese, the Tonkinese should not show too much of an inclination towards either of these foundation breeds, but be a happy medium of the two, like this Lilac.

✦ LEFT
A Blue Tonkinese has the required light aquamarine eyes. Siamese blue or Burmese chartreuse are considered faults.

BREED BOX	
Coat	short, close-lying, fine, soft, silky with a lustrous sheen
Eyes	almond-shaped, slightly slanted; aquamarine
Grooming	easy; regular, gentle brushing
Temperament	equable, lively, inquisitive, relaxed, very friendly

◆ LEFT
The mixture of brown, red and cream in a Brown Tortie Tonkinese needs to be well mingled and should darken at the points to meet the exacting standards set for the breed.

tendency to stoutness of the Burmese. Ears are large with rounded tips. The coat pattern shades to a darker tone on the legs, ears, mask and tail. Coat colour too, is a compromise – paler than Burmese but darker than Siamese. The cat has a calm temperament but with a streak of mischief and the welcome addition of hybrid vigour.

It is very important for the point colour to be definitely darker than the main body colour on mask, ears, legs and tail, but without any sharp colour changes such as those seen in the Siamese. Underparts should be lighter than the upper body, which in turn should show gradation of tone rather than sudden changes.

The eye colour of the Tonkinese is neither the startling amber nor chartreuse green found in the Burmese, nor the deep sapphire of the Siamese. It can range from aquamarine blue to greenish-blue or bluish-green. It may take some time for eye colour to settle. Tonkinese generally mature slowly, reaching their final colouring and peak size at about two years of age.

TONKINESE COLOURS AND PATTERNS

Solid colours	Brown, Blue, Chocolate, Lilac, Red, Cream, Caramel, Apricot
Tortoiseshell	Brown, Blue, Chocolate, Lilac, Caramel
Tabby	Brown, Blue, Chocolate, Lilac, Red, Cream, Caramel, Apricot
Tortie Tabby	Brown, Blue, Chocolate, Lilac, Caramel

In the United States the breed is recognized in Natural Mink, Champagne Mink, Blue Mink, Platinum Mink and Honey Mink

◆ BELOW
This Blue Tabby is a typical example of the Siamese ancestry being too obvious in its extended limbs and slim line. It may not win show prizes, but is nevertheless a beautiful animal.

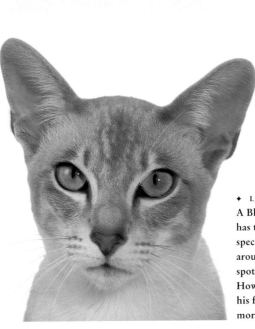

◆ LEFT
A Blue Tabby Tonkinese has the preferred spectacle-like rings around its eyes and spotted whisker pads. However, the M shape on his forehead could be more distinct.

EGYPTIAN MAU

On ancient Egyptian manuscripts and murals, a cat is depicted that looks very much like the modern breed of Egyptian Mau. The breeder wanted to replicate the cats of the Pharaohs, and founded the breeding line from a native Egyptian breed that seemed to have evolved spontaneously in the Cairo region. The first Egyptian Mau (the name is ancient Egyptian for a sacred domestic cat) kitten was shown in Rome in the 1950s. Its owner emigrated with her cats to America, where the breed was granted recognition by the Cat Fanciers' Association in 1977. It is now available in Silver (charcoal markings on silver), Bronze, and Smoke (black markings on charcoal/silver underlay) varieties. The Bronze, with dark brown to black markings on a warm bronze undercoat, is closest in appearance to the cat depicted on Egyptian murals. Europe did not recognize the breed

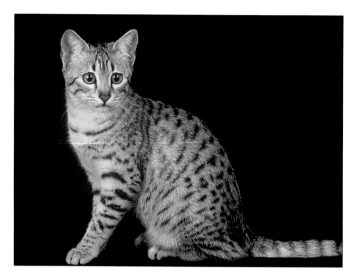

◆ LEFT
Spotted cats very similar to this were illustrated in ancient Egyptian manuscripts and murals. The M-shaped mark on its brow is said to echo the pattern on the back of the scarab beetle, which was sacred to the Egyptians.

until 1992. A spotted cat bred from Siamese lines in England during the 1960s was originally called Egyptian Mau, but later became established as the Oriental Spotted Tabby.

The Egyptian Mau is a medium-sized, muscular cat, pleasing to the eye, easy to groom, and with an extrovert personality. It tends to bond with just one or two people, and is not averse to learning a trick or two, or to walking on a lead. Its head is slightly oriental in shape, with large, alert ears, although its muzzle is well rounded. The conformation is generally graceful, with hind legs slightly longer than the front legs, and a well-balanced tail.

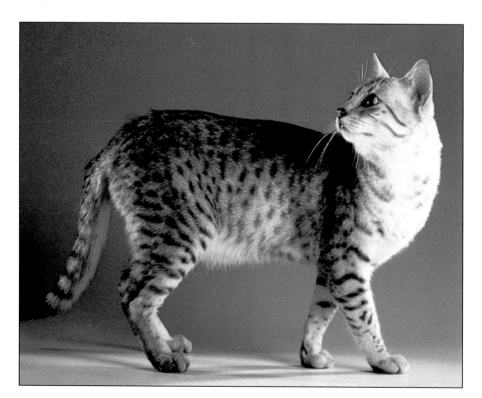

BREED BOX	
Coat	medium length, dense, lustrous, silky
Eyes	large, alert, almond-shaped, slightly slanted; light green
Other features	spotted coat
Grooming	easy; regular gentle brushing to remove dead hairs
Temperament	affectionate, lively; may be aloof

◆ LEFT
The well-defined spots are the most important features of the Mau. This Bronze is probably the closest in colour to its Egyptian forebears.

SINGAPURA

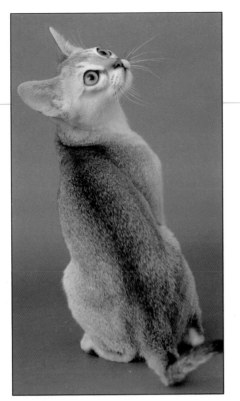

♦ LEFT
The Singapura is one of the few breeds that is only available in one colour, a warm ivory overlaid with sepia-brown ticking. This one shows characteristic darker shading along the length of its spine.

During the early 1970s, an experienced and influential American cat breeder found a colony of unusual looking cats in Singapore. How they had come to be in a feral state is not known, although there is ample evidence that the cat that came to be known as the Singapura had existed for a long time. Because of the feral state in which they were found, the cats were known as drain or river cats. At one time, they were culled by the Singaporean authorities. Now the Malay government has adopted the animal as the country's national cat, and renamed it *Kucinta*, which means love cat.

The Singapura is on the small side, but stocky and muscular. Its head is round, its ears are large, wide-based and pointed at the top; its eyes are huge. The neck is thick and short, the muzzle broad, and the nose blunt. The nose and eyes are further accentuated by dark eye-liner outlines.

The characteristic Singapura coat is that of a ticked tabby with some markings on the back of the legs, but not on the front. Its usual colour is called sepia agouti, which is dark brown ticking on an old-ivory ground.

The Singapura quickly took a very firm hold on European affections, and is on its way to becoming an established championship breed.

♦ LEFT
Owl-like eyes are a particular feature of the Singapura, orbs of gold and green fetchingly outlined in black.

♦ BELOW
Small but perfectly formed could be an apt description of the Singapura, but the cats are well-muscled and feel much heavier than they look.

BREED BOX

Coat	fine, short, close-lying
Eyes	large, rounded almond-shaped; brilliant colour
Other features	huge eyes on small frame
Grooming	very easy; regular brushing
Temperament	affectionate, good-natured, gentle, playful

OCICAT

The Ocicat is one of the glorious accidents in the cat fancy. A breeder from the state of Michigan in the United States set out to create a Ticked Point Siamese. She mated a Siamese with an Abyssinian. One of the offspring was mated back to another Siamese male, and a tabby Point Siamese duly appeared. However, one kitten was ivory-coated with clear golden spots. This was the very first Ocicat, its name inspired by the wild ocelot, because of the similarity in coat colour and pattern. Many breeders used the same breeding

This Chocolate Silver Ocicat shows all the finer points required of the breed, including hindquarters that are rather higher than the front.

♦ BELOW
At birth, the Ocicat kitten may have a very indistinct pattern. The spots develop as the cat matures, and this 15-week-old kitten is looking promising.

BREED BOX

Coat	short, thick, smooth and satiny with lustrous sheen
Eyes	large, slanted, almond-shaped; all colours except blue
Other features	spotted coat
Grooming	easy; regular brushing
Temperament	affectionate, active

♦ ABOVE
There should be a clear M mark on the forehead of Ocicats, but this is less obvious in the dilute colours such as this Lilac.

♦ ABOVE
The spotting on the coat of the Ocicat should be well defined – faint or blurred spots are a serious fault, even on the less contrasted colours of the Lilac and other dilute forms.

formula successfully. Recognition was granted in the United States in the 1960s, although championship status was not achieved until 1987. Preliminary recognition in the United Kingdom did not come until 1998. Ocicats are now available in Brown, Blue,

Chocolate, Lilac, Cinnamon, and Fawn, as well as the Silver-based versions of these colours. A few authorities also recognize Red, Cream and Tortoiseshell. It is a long-bodied, well-muscled animal, with medium-length legs and a long, tapered tail. It has a round head with a prominent muzzle and large, pointed ears.

♦ BELOW
A Chocolate Ocicat displays an intelligent and friendly disposition – a blend of character and temperament inherited from the breed's original Abyssinian and Siamese parentage.

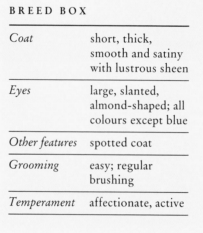

JAPANESE BOBTAIL

There are representations of the Japanese Bobtail on ancient prints and manuscripts dating back some 2,000 years. On the Gotojuki temple in Tokyo, built during the Edo period (1615–1867), is a famous portrayal of a beckoning Bobtail.

Legend has it that a cat in Japan was warming itself in front of a fire when it accidentally set its tail alight. It ran through the city and spread the fire through the fragile wooden houses, which were burnt to ashes. The Emperor of Japan decreed all cats should be punished and ordered their tails to be chopped off. There is a similar story surrounding the origin of Manx cats.

What actually caused this particular gene mutation is a mystery. Unlike the Manx, the mating of two Japanese Bobtails will produce only more Japanese Bobtails.

An American who lived in Japan after World War II returned to the United States with 38 Bobtails to found a breeding line. Provisional

◆ ABOVE
A Red and White Japanese Bobtail shows that, unlike the tailless true Manx, the breed has a very short tail that curls around its rump.

BREED BOX

Coat	Shorthair: medium in length, soft and silky with no undercoat Longhair: medium to long, soft and silky with no undercoat; frontal ruff desirable
Eyes	large, oval; colour reflects coat colour
Other features	short, moveable tail
Grooming	easy; regular combing
Temperament	affectionate, intelligent, inquisitive, needs attention

status was granted in 1971, and championship status in 1976. Japanese breeders began to develop a long-coated variation in 1954, although the type had unofficially been around for centuries, particularly in the northern regions of Japan. They were represented in ancient Japanese paintings, but had been ignored by the pedigree cat aficionados. They were recognized in 1991 by The International Cat Association.

The Japanese Bobtail is a medium-sized cat with clean lines and bone structure. It is well muscled but straight and slender rather than massive in build. The set of the eyes combined with high cheek-bones, lends a distinctive cast to the face, especially in profile, which is quite different from other oriental breeds. Its short tail should resemble a rabbit tail, with the hair fanning out to create a pompon appearance which effectively camouflages the underlying bone structure.

The cats are now available in most colours and patterns. In Japan, they are thought of as bringing good fortune to a household, especially the van-patterned Tortie and White, known as the mi-ke (three colours).

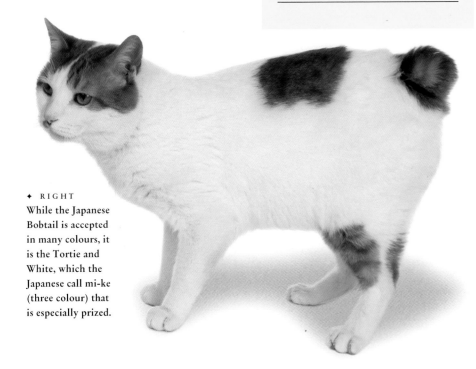

◆ RIGHT
While the Japanese Bobtail is accepted in many colours, it is the Tortie and White, which the Japanese call mi-ke (three colour) that is especially prized.

MANX

A colony of cats became stranded on an island off the west coast of mainland Britain and eventually formed a distinct type. One myth suggests that the tailless Manx cat originated from a mating between a rabbit and a cat; another that the cat was the last to leave Noah's Ark and had its tail chopped in the door. The reality is that the Isle of Man cat community was forced by its confinement into concentrated interbreeding. A mutant gene that led to a spinal malformation spread throughout the community and became the norm. The spine was literally curtailed, ending (in what is described as a true or rumpy Manx) in a hollow where a tail should have been. Cats with brief stumps of tails were also born, and these are called stumpies, stubbies or risers. The gene that causes this condition is related to

BREED BOX

Coat	double, well-padded
Eyes	large, round; colour in keeping with coat colour
Other features	lack of tail
Grooming	easy; regular brushing
Temperament	calm, intelligent, active, loyal; likes to be with its owner

◆ ABOVE
A residual tail is just visible on the Black Manx, which means that he cannot qualify as a true Manx on the show circuit. He will, however, be valuable for breeding purposes.

◆ ABOVE
The strong features typical of the Manx are evident on this Red Spotted Tabby. His cheeks are full, ears are prominent and his nose is broad, straight and of medium length.

◆ LEFT
A true, or rumpy, Manx has a hollow where its tail should be. This Tortoiseshell Tabby and White shows the stocky build typical of the breed. The chest is broad, and the back short. The rump is higher than the shoulder.

◆ LEFT
Manx cats have now been bred in all standard colours and patterns except colourpointed (Himalayan). This is a Blue-Cream rumpy, showing the required absolute lack of tail; it should be completely rounded with no definite rise of bone or cartilage.

the one that causes spina bifida in humans. If male and female rumpies are mated, some of the foetuses may not develop to full term. Breeders therefore introduce part- or fully-tailed varieties into their breeding programmes. For show purposes,

however, it is the taillessness of the rumpy that is accepted as the standard for the breed. It is accepted in all the standard colours and patterns except colourpointed, although Lilac and Chocolate are not recognized by some associations.

◆ ABOVE
Note the front legs of this Manx Bi-colour. They are slightly shorter than the long, muscular hind legs which result in a characteristic rabbit-like, loping gait.

MANX CAT VARIETIES

Rumpy shows a hollow where the tail should emerge. This is the Manx cat exhibited at cat shows

Rumpy Riser has few fused vertebrae at the end of the spine. These can be seen and definitely felt, which disqualifies the cat from being shown as a Manx. It is, however, used for breeding

Stumpy has a very short tail that can be moved. The vertebrae are not necessarily fused. This is the form which gives rise to some of the bobtailed cats

Longy has an almost normal length tail. Often these cats are indistinguishable from the normal domestic feline

Cymric is a rare semi-longhair variety, which is described in the Semi-longhair section of this book

◆ BELOW
The occasional tailed Manx is born of Manx parents. He or she will win no prizes for Manx type perfection, but with the typical bulkiness of the type and a freedom from the spinal defects, is an extremely valuable asset to any Manx breeding programme.

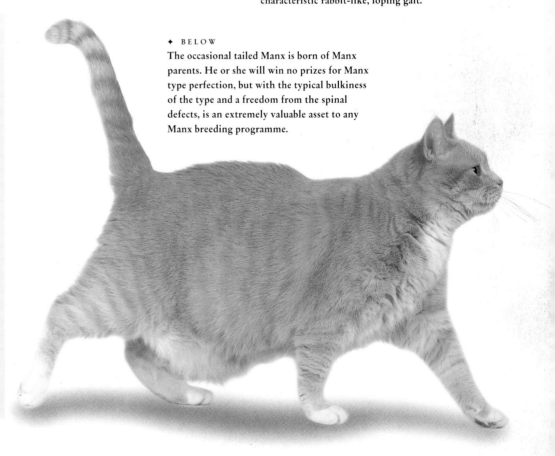

REX CATS

The distinguishing feature of all Rex cats is their waved coat pattern. Rex fur grows at a much slower rate than the fur on most cats, and is the way it is because it is less developed. Most cats, both longhairs and shorthairs, have three levels of hair – a fine down undercoat, a layer of bristly awn hairs, and outer guardhairs. On Rex cats (with the exception of the Selkirk Rex) the outer guardhairs are usually non-existent, and the awn hairs are much shorter than usual, resulting in a fine, downy coat that tends to wave or curl. Even the whiskers of a Rex are shorter than is usual.

Another characteristic shared by most Rex cats is their athleticism. They have compact, muscular bodies, and are notably active and agile. Nevertheless, they are ready to bond strongly with their owners and are more likely than many cats to take to going for walks on a lead. The name rex is taken from a curly-coated rabbit of the same name. A geneticist compared the fur of the Cornish Rex cat and the Rex rabbit and found the genetic make-up of each to be similar.

The various Rex breeds are all quite distinct, and were discovered and developed quite independently of each other. They were all, however, due to spontaneously occurring mutant genes. They were named after the regions in which they were discovered.

German Rex cats (which have slighter denser fur) were first bred specifically in East Berlin just after World War II. Ohio and Oregon Rex cats, which were discovered in the states of the same names, do not appear to have survived as breeding lines.

◆ TOP AND ABOVE
Compare the facial characteristics of the Devon Rex (*top*) and Cornish Rex (*above*). The Cornish breed has a longer face, while the Devon Rex has prominent cheek-bones and very large ears.

◆ BELOW
The Cornish Rex, with its crisply waved coat, is now available in all colours and patterns, from self colours, to this White and Black Smoke, and all the various colourpoints.

CORNISH REX

The first recorded Cornish Rex kitten was born in 1950 in Cornwall, England, to a plain-coated tortoiseshell and white female. The kitten was a cream classic tabby with white chest and white belly. Its fur was closely waved. It was mated with its mother, and the resulting litter contained two curly-coated kittens. Because of the close interbreeding of the early Cornish Rexes, the gene pool was restricted and the kittens became weaker. Most of the kittens had to be put down, but one survivor, the son of one of the original kittens, was mated to his daughter before she was exported to the United States. Her lineage was strengthened by outcrossed matings with other breeds, and then back-crossed to rex cats to recreate the recessive curly coat. The breed was officially recognized in 1967.

The Cornish Rex has an elongated wedge of a head that curves gently at the forehead. The muzzle is rounded, the chin strong and the profile straight. The ears are startlingly large. The body is hard and muscular, with the legs long and straight, and the tail fine and tapering. The Cornish Rex comes in all colours, patterns and colour combinations.

BREED BOX	
Coat	short, plushy, silky; no guardhairs; waves, curls or ripples particularly on back and tail
Eyes	medium, oval
Other features	big ears
Grooming	gentle brushing, using fingers to set waves
Temperament	intelligent, thoughtful, active

DEVON REX

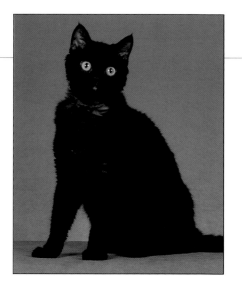

◆ LEFT
The Devon Rex is affectionately described as having a pixie-like expression – which reflects its mischievous character.

In 1960, another curly-coated cat was discovered in Devon, England, the neighbouring county to the home of the Cornish Rex. A curly-coated feral male had mated with a stray, straight-haired female, and the litter included one curly-coated male. As the curly hair gene is recessive and needs to find a matching one to emerge, the female must have had a compatible gene pool. However, the gene which caused the coat was quite different from that of the Cornish Rex – mating the two breeds resulted in only straight-coated offspring.

The Devon Rex coat is generally less dense than that of the Cornish Rex and, without careful breeding, very sparse coats can result. Physically, the Devon Rex is quite different from the Cornish. It shares the muscular build, slim legs and long, whip-like tail, but it is broad chested, and has a flat forehead, prominent cheek-bones and a crinkled brow. All coat colours, patterns and colour combinations are allowed.

BREED BOX

Coat	very short, fine, wavy, soft; can have a rippled effect
Eyes	wide-set, large and oval; all colours
Grooming	requires very gentle stroking with a soft mitt rather than a brush
Temperament	extraordinarily playful; mischievous yet never unkind

SELKIRK REX

A curly-coated tortoiseshell and white kitten was born in a humane society in Wyoming in the United States in 1987. It was mated to top-quality Persian breeding lines and the offspring crossed back to the distinctive curly-coated line. The resulting Selkirk Rex embraces both long- and shorthaired cats. The Selkirk Rex Breed Club has stipulated that no outcrosses should be made to other Rex breeds, so that the line retains a strong identity. Only one Selkirk Rex parent is necessary for some rexed kittens to be produced.

The Selkirk Rex has denser fur than other Rex breeds, including guardhairs. Build is stocky and rectangular, but with a rounded head and wide cheeks. The breed was accepted for registration by the American Cat Fanciers' Association in 1992 but is not recognized in the United Kingdom.

BREED BOX

Coat	lambswool texture, with curled guard- and awn hairs; thick and dense
Eyes	round, full, wide-set; all colours
Grooming	gentle and regular with a wide-toothed comb
Temperament	calm, affectionate, playful

◆ ABOVE AND RIGHT
Persian cats introduced into the breeding line mean that the Selkirk Rex has a full body of fur, unlike the other Rex breeds. There are shorthair varieties, such as this Black Smoke (*above*), and longhairs like the Silver Chocolate Lynx Point (*right*).

AMERICAN CURL

Early in the 1980s, a stray kitten with strange, backwardly reflexed ears, was discovered in California. Two curly-eared kittens were born to this stray, one shorthaired, the other longhaired. The breed – for this birth heralded the start of the American Curl's rise to fame and fortune – has therefore always had the two coat options. The two kittens were shown at a local show, and the response was electric. It is very rare for the big cat associations to take up a new breed so rapidly, but that is precisely what happened. The American Curl was granted recognition by The International Cat

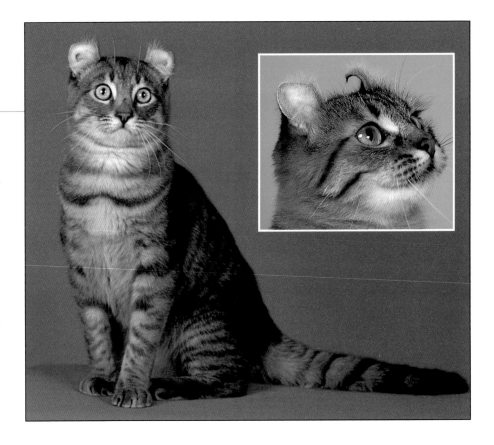

✦ ABOVE
A Blue Mackerel Tabby demonstrates the well-balanced conformation of the American Curl – to match the breed's evenness of temperament.

✦ INSET ABOVE
The extraordinary shape of the American Curl's ear can be fully appreciated in this Brown Mackerel Tabby.

✦ LEFT
A strikingly marked Brown Mac Tabby pricks up its distinctive ears. Ideally, they should curve back in a smooth arc of at least 90 degrees but not more than 180 degrees, and have rounded and flexible tips.

BREED BOX

Coat	long or short; both are silky, lying flat without plushiness
Eyes	large, walnut-shaped; all colours
Other features	ears curled back
Grooming	relatively easy; regular brushing; check ears
Temperament	eager to please; needs attention

✦ BELOW
Because the breeding line was founded on a pair of kittens which were both curly-eared but had different coat lengths, there are longhaired American Curls, too, as this Red Classic Tabby shows.

✦ RIGHT
Not only do American Curls come in two coat lengths, but there is now a wide choice of colours and patterns. This magnificent cat is a Brown Mac Tabby and White longhair.

Association in 1985, followed by the Cat Fanciers' Association in 1986. It is a winsomely charming cat with ears that curve backwards as though windswept, or the cat is listening very carefully to something just behind it.

The ears should be wide at the base and open. Otherwise, the breed is medium-sized, well-balanced and well-muscled. The legs are medium length with round paws, and the tail is flexible and tapering, equal to body length. The American Curl comes in all colours, patterns and colour combinations.

No other anomalies or physical defects have occurred in the breed, and successful outcrossing to other breeds is continuing to ensure that a strong, healthy type is maintained. However, as yet, the breed is not recognized in the United Kingdom, being rejected on the same grounds as the Scottish Fold.

SCOTTISH FOLD

One day in 1961, a Scottish farmer spotted a little white cat with strangely folded ears. A year later, this cat produced other folded-ear kittens. A British Blue Shorthair was introduced into what had become the foundations

✦ LEFT
Although its country of origin is Scotland, the Scottish Fold is relatively unknown in the United Kingdom, although popular in the United States. Its downward folding ears emphasize the roundness of its head.

BREED BOX

Coat	short, dense, plush
Eyes	wide-set, large, round
Other features	ears folded forward
Grooming	relatively easy; regular brushing; check ears
Temperament	a self-assured cat and, because of its British Shorthair and Persian antecedents, generally placid, independent yet very loving

of the Scottish Fold. However, it was discovered that the gene that caused the folded ears was dominant, and could also cause skeletal problems in some cats. The Governing Council of the Cat Fancy in the United Kingdom, among others, has resisted recognition of the breed because of the risk of a kitten being born with skeletal abnormalities. This may occur even if a Fold is mated with another, proven breed. The Scottish Fold, found in a wide range of coats and patterns, is a medium-sized cat, which may be short- or longhaired. It has a round head held on a short neck and its nose is short with a gentle curve. Despite short legs, the cat is not inactive.

AMERICAN WIREHAIR

◆ BELOW

Apart from its curly coat and whiskers, the American Wirehair is very much like its compatriot, the American Shorthair.

The coat of the American Wirehair – which, as its name suggests, is its most distinguishing feature – is by no means fully rexed, but it is far more crimped, crinkled and bouncy than that of most cats. The origins of the breed go back to a barn in Upper New York State in 1966. A red and white curly-coated male occurred as a spontaneous mutation in an American Shorthair litter. By 1969, a pure-breeding colony had been established, and the breed was given official recognition by the Cat

BREED BOX

Coat	springy, tight, medium in length; individual hairs are crimped, hooked or bent
Eyes	wide-set, large, round; all colours
Grooming	minimal with an occasional soft brushing
Temperament	very positive and inquisitive; they never seem to stop purring

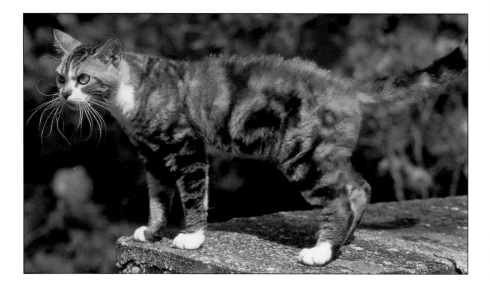

Fanciers' Association in 1978. The breed remains more or less exclusively in the United States, but there was a class for American Wirehairs at a Brussels show in 1996.

It is a medium to large cat with a round head, prominent cheek-bones and a well-developed muzzle. It comes in all colours and patterns except the colourpointed (Himalayan) series.

SPHYNX

Hairless cats were supposedly bred by the Aztec people of Central America hundreds of years ago. The last pair of cats of this Mexican breed was presented to an American couple by Pueblo Indians in Albuquerque, New Mexico in 1903. Unfortunately, the male was savaged to death by a pack of dogs and so the breed did not survive. The modern Sphynx breeding programme began in 1966 in Toronto,

◆ ABOVE

The face of a Black Tortie Tabby shows the high cheek-bones, well-defined whisker pads, and backward-slanting, lemon-shaped eyes of the breed.

◆ LEFT

A Black and White Bi-colour Sphynx demonstrates the breed's long, slender neck, very large ears and very short whiskers. The breed is sometimes referred to as the ET of the cat world.

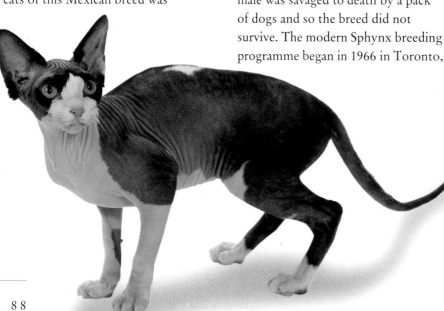

BREED BOX

Coat	a fine body suede
Eyes	large, slightly slanted
Other features	wrinkled skin at key points, few or no whiskers; big ears, whip-like tail
Grooming	fairly easy; more sponging and wiping than combing and brushing
Temperament	intelligent, very lively and playful

+ LEFT
It is acceptable for a Sphynx to have wrinkled folds of skin around its neck and legs, but it should be smooth elsewhere, like this Brown Tabby.

Canada, when an ordinary shorthaired, black and white domestic cat bore a hairless male kitten. An expert breeder bought mother and son and developed the breed from there.

The Sphynx is not exactly hairless; its skin is covered with a soft, warm down which feels like the furred skin of a peach. There may be visible fur on the brow, around the toes and at the tip of the tail. Otherwise, it is a well-built, sturdy cat with a head slightly longer than it is wide, set on a long, slender neck. The large wide-open ears are tall and the outer edge is in line with the wedge of the face. Cheek-bones are prominent, and in profile there is a distinct break at the bridge of the nose. It has long, slim legs with elegant yet rounded paws – the toes are long, like little fingers – and a long, finely tapered tail.

The skin needs regular and careful cleaning, as the cat perspires and a greasy detritus can build up if neglected, which then has to be scraped or sponged away. The cat is also prone to skin allergies and to developing lumps. However, humans who are normally allergic to cats may find they can tolerate the furless Sphynx.

The breed has been refused recognition by some registering associations on the grounds that its genetic constitution is a malformation. However, it does have official recognition from The International Cat Association as well as independent clubs in Europe, and there is a flourishing group of Sphynx breeders in Belgium and the Netherlands.

+ ABOVE
This little chap is a Harlequin Sphynx. All colours and patterns are now available in the breed. Although it is not currently accepted in Britain, it has a firm following in North America and is gaining popularity in Europe.

+ BELOW
This Blue shows the remarkable, sleek bodyline of the breed. The cats are lithe and muscular, with accompanying energy and playfulness.

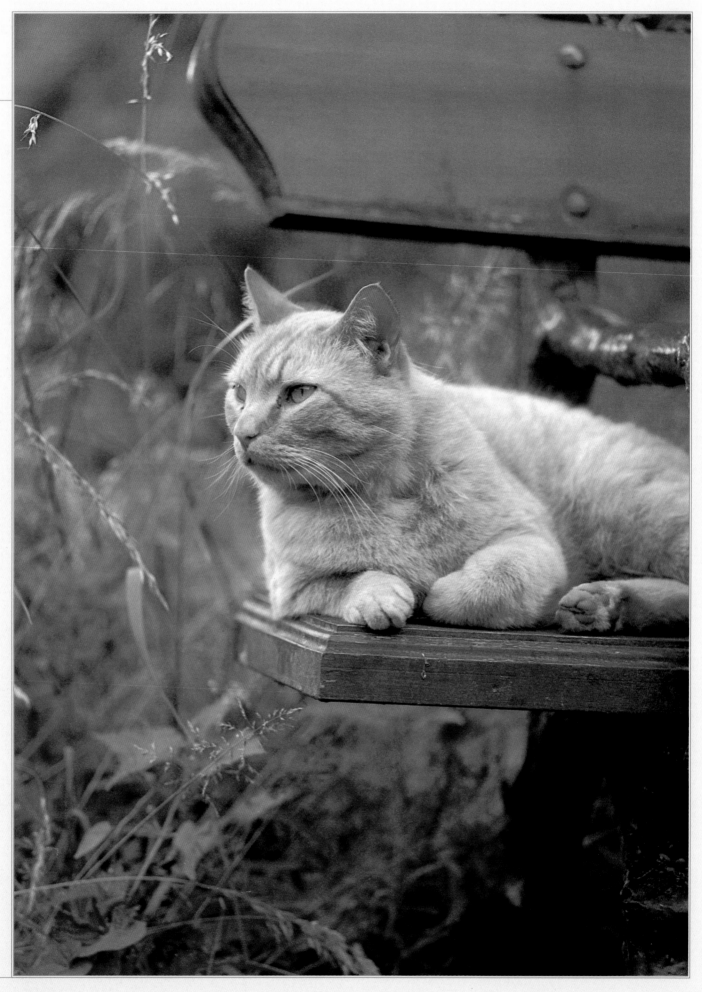

Non-pedigreed Cats

A cat does not have to have an impressive pedigree to bring feline quality into our lives. Non-pedigreed cats with unknown parentage can have just as much grace and beauty as the finest show specimens. However, as there are endless possible combinations of sire and dam in a non-pedigreed ancestry, the appearance and character of what emerges is something of a lottery.

◆ FACING PAGE
An ordinary ginger tom looks perfectly contented with his non-pedigreed lineage, and is probably allowed more freedom to roam than his high-bred equivalent would be.

◆ ABOVE
It may not win any prizes for symmetry of fur pattern, but this black and white non-pedigree could be entered in the household pet category of a cat show.

AN ORDINARY CAT

Non-pedigreed cats – also known as household pets, domestic cats or random-bred – are the most common cats kept as pets. Fewer than five per cent of pet cats have a pedigree.

Acquiring a non-pedigree is far easier and cheaper than buying a purebred cat. Rescue organizations and humane societies are overflowing with animals all ready to make ideal companions, and some are as beautiful as their purebred equivalents. It is unlikely that such a cat will cost more than a donation to the society and the cost of vaccinations.

The disadvantage of having a non-pedigreed animal is that you invariably do not know what you are getting, whereas a quality guarantee comes with a pedigree. Because of their mixed ancestry, non-pedigrees are usually intelligent and affectionate, but a bad character gene could slip in.

COMMON HERITAGE
Both pedigreed and pet cats have common ancestors in the

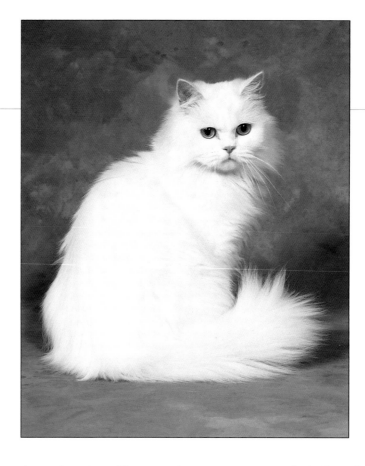

♦ LEFT
Would you like a very expensive White Persian or Balinese, or would this extraordinarily pretty non-pedigreed longhaired white do just as well?

domesticated cat. However, the pedigree has evolved as a result of selective breeding, while the pet cat conforms to no special standards except those dictated by evolutionary pressures and the need to survive.

Non-pedigreed cats may have coats of any length and in a range of colours that are usually plain, blotched, striped or patched. Cats of one colour are less common than tabbies, bi-colours and tortoiseshells, and may indicate an unplanned mating with a pedigreed partner. Eyes are usually green or yellow and the majority of non-pedigreed noses are fairly long.

OFF-THE-STREET OPTIONS
You could, literally, pick your non-pedigree up off the street. Non-neutered (unaltered) mongrel cats roam all over the place, breeding prolifically. The resulting unwanted litters add to a population of feral cats – those that have been born in the wild or that have reverted to the wild state. Some, like those found by the hundred on Greek islands, tread a fine line between wildness and domesticity. Such cats present enormous problems for rescue organizations (if they exist), but have the potential for providing all the qualities looked for in the pet cat. They can be socialized, but the owner has to spend as much time with the cat as possible, particularly during

♦ BELOW
If your bank balance cannot stretch to the cost of a Maine Coon Cat or Norwegian Forest Cat, this well-whiskered, soft ginger semi-longhair might suffice.

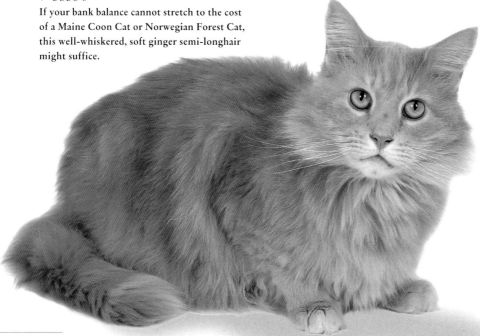

◆ BELOW
It looks as if there is a touch of Persian in this short-nosed, cobby ginger, and he seems to have inherited some of the Persian placidity as well.

the first few weeks. Medical examination and inoculations are also particularly important.

NEAR MISSES
For something a little more refined, you could go for a cat that only just misses being a pedigree. In one tiny, isolated community, there was only one local unneutered (unaltered) tom – which was clearly the sire of a litter produced by a neighbouring purebred Lilac Point Siamese queen. Four of her kittens were lilac-pointed (albeit with slightly longer, coarser hair than their pedigreed mother), and the fifth looked like a Black Oriental Shorthair. Nonetheless, they were all non-pedigree. Fortunately, they had inherited the best of their mother's oriental looks and their father's robust health and character.

Other non-pedigrees have known ancestry too. Farm cats may have bred for generations. Some kittens would be selected and kept because they were prettier, more intelligent, or had better mouse-catching potential than others. If the owners kept a record of the these kittens' parentage, they would be founding a written pedigree. That is how the pedigree system began.

SHOW STANDARD PETS
Many cat shows have Non-pedigree or Household Pet classes. There are no set standards of hair length, colour or conformation as there are with the pedigreed breeds. The cats are judged on their general appeal – their friendliness, beauty and condition.

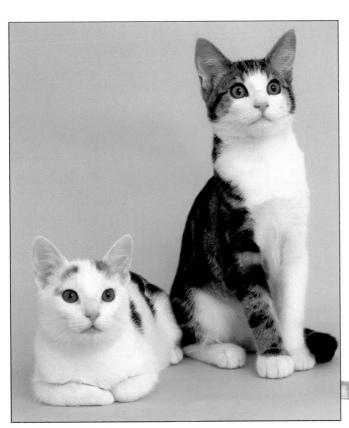

◆ LEFT
Any coat length and colour combination is possible in the non-pedigreed range. What these two shorthairs lack in irregular coat pattern they make up for in alertness and pretty, balanced features.

◆ RIGHT
A well-defined blaze, chest and paws would be desirable in a pedigreed bi-colour, but with this non-pedigree, character would be a more important factor if it were to be entered in a show.

Breeding from Your Cat

The vast majority of people are quite content to own a cat, or cats, and leave it at that. Their animals are neutered (altered) and live the life of non-reproductive felines that simply grace the lives and homes of their owner. There are other people who become deeply involved in breeding cats as a hobby – it is rarely a profitable business. The amateur cat breeder may be rewarded by a handful of exquisite and charming kittens that may or may not be perfect pedigrees, but he or she is also taking on an expensive, time-absorbing, and often frustrating commitment.

♦ FACING PAGE
A Singapura mother and her kitten demonstrate the rewards of breeding in their beauty and character. The breed was developed from the "drain cats" of Singapore.

♦ ABOVE
A pale coat combined with darker points at ears, nose, tail and paws – seen to great effect in the Siamese – is known in breeding circles as the "Himalayan factor".

THE REWARDS OF BREEDING

◆ BELOW
The ultimate reward for a breeder is to produce a pedigreed cat of such perfection of type and temperament that it becomes a national Supreme Grand Champion like the Cream Colourpoint Longhair, Rosjoy Rambo.

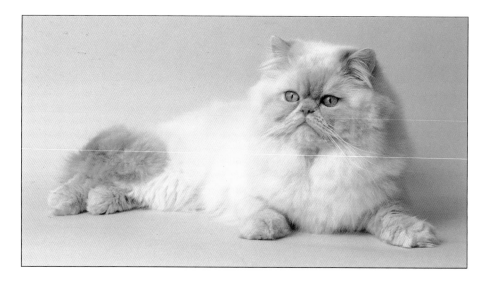

Think carefully of the implications before you decide to let your cat have kittens. Whether you are giving your non-pedigree a chance to be a mother before having her neutered (altered), or planning to propagate a pedigree line, the process can be both time-consuming and expensive. Perhaps the most important consideration of all is to be sure that you will be able to find good homes for the kittens. If not, or if the prospective buyers change their minds, you must be prepared to give them a permanent home yourself.

Most people who breed from their cats are dealing with pedigrees rather than random-bred animals, with a view to continuing or improving on pure-bred lines. For the cat lover, the pedigree cat world is one of absorbing interest and beauty. It is also a stimulating environment where you will learn a great deal; your rivals will often become your best friends.

THE COMMITMENT

Those who go into breeding pedigrees thinking they are going to earn a lot of money from selling them are going to be disappointed. Even the most experienced and reputable breeders are lucky to break even over the course of any financial year. There are veterinary bills to pay for both mother and offspring, stud fees, special diets for the pregnant and nursing mother, heating for the kittens, veterinary testing and inoculation, and registration and advertising costs.

A heavily pregnant and nursing cat needs attention. The queen may not deliver her kittens at a convenient time and place during the day. This may happen in the early hours of the morning, and she may need some help from you, especially if it is her first litter. There may be deaths to deal with, especially in a first litter, which will be extremely distressing for everyone concerned.

Kittens may be lovable and cute, but they can also be destructive and get in the way. They need to be watched and cared for, and prepared for going out into the world. You should raise a pedigree litter for love and interest rather than money, and preferably when you already have some experience as an owner.

HOW IT ALL BEGAN

Breeding pedigreed cats on a serious level did not take place until the 1800s. The first cat show, held in London in 1871, set a trend for exhibiting, which in turn led to a more calculated approach to breeding. The organizer, an artist and author called Harrison Weir, set guidelines for breeding which became the basis for standards throughout the world, although different countries set their own rules. Most of the cats in the early shows were domestic shorthairs and Persians.

◆ BELOW
After a particularly awful day, with kittens into everything and apparently multiplying, many a cat breeder wonders, "Why am I doing this?" One look at this trio of bi-colours would probably answer the question.

✦ BELOW
Diminutive yet powerful Singapuras are the
pedigreed version of the Singapore alley cat. The
best examples were selected and bred to produce
a pedigree which is increasing in popularity.

✦ BELOW
If your breeding
programme produces
a line-up of six week-
old Blue and Cream
Persians, like this
one, you should have
no difficulty finding
a home for them.

It was not until the 1880s that Asian breeds were introduced to western Europe. The first Siamese cats were exhibited in Britain in 1885. By this time, breeders in Europe and America were setting up their own breeding programmes. They drew from the best British pedigreed stock and their own indigenous cats. The first American cat show was in New York in 1895.

A NEW BREED
There are now more than fifty internationally recognized breeds, and several others that are recognized as established and distinct breeds in some countries but not in others. The purpose of breeding may go beyond a desire to produce kittens for show or for sale, or even to keep a pedigree line going. Careful and well-informed selection of the queen and the stud can improve the type. Instead of waiting for the natural processes of evolution to select the fittest of a species, a breeder can speed up the process. Picking the healthiest and most well-formed examples of indigenous street cats, and mating them, for example, led to the development of standard types of British, American and European shorthairs. Breeders can also try to create a new variety of cat – a new colour variation of an established breed, or a new breed altogether. However, this is an area that should be left to the experts who have built up an in-depth knowledge of feline genetics, for mutations do sometimes occur. To establish a new breed takes many years. Only after several matings can a breed be proved to produce healthy offspring of consistent type, and only then be officially registered.

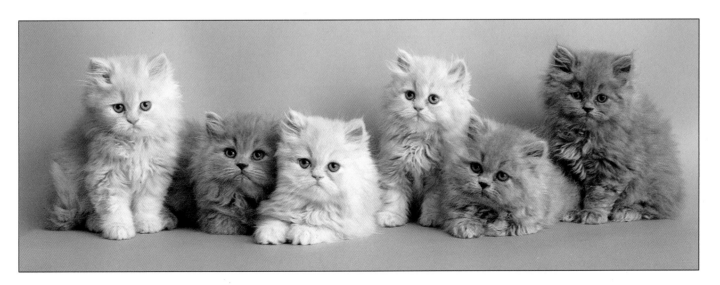

ACQUIRING A QUEEN

Choosing the breed and pedigree line you are going to use to found your breeding programme requires preparation and in-depth research. Gather as much information as you can about your chosen breed and study the genetics of breeding from specialist books and magazines, and from the individual breed clubs.

Unless you are going to breed with a cat you already own, it is sensible to look for suitably pedigreed parents and book a female kitten from their next litter. This kitten will, after all, be the foundation of your breeding line. She should be of the best standard and pedigree that you can afford.

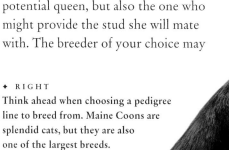

AIMING HIGH

In any event, you should not select a kitten you are planning to breed from until it is at least three months old. By this time you will be able to assess its personality, and the colouring and patterns of its coat. The national cat-registering bodies, such as the Governing Council of the Cat Fancy in the United Kingdom and the Cat Fanciers' Association in the United States, publish set standards of perfection for each registered breed. These not only help you identify suitable parents for your own breeding female, but give you, as a breeder, clear guidelines to aim for.

Individual breed clubs have lists of breeders from whom you can buy your female. Visit cat shows, too – either those for individual breeds or large national shows where the whole range of registered breeds can be seen. Many championship and specialist breed shows take place throughout the year. You can obtain

details of shows from the breed clubs and national registering organizations. Breeders and exhibitors at cat shows are usually delighted to talk about their animals.

The early contacts you make at clubs and shows are vital first steps in joining the cat-breeding network. You may find not only the breeder from whom you will acquire your own potential queen, but also the one who might provide the stud she will mate with. The breeder of your choice may

✦ ABOVE
The majority of breeders in the United Kingdom keep their breeding queens as family pets.

✦ RIGHT
Think ahead when choosing a pedigree line to breed from. Maine Coons are splendid cats, but they are also one of the largest breeds.

not have any kittens at the time you want one, but is likely to know of someone else who does.

BEYOND APPEARANCES

You will initially be attracted by the outward physical appearance of a particular breed or cat. However, when you are considering breeding, it is particularly important to look for animals with responsive and outgoing yet calm natures. This generally indicates that they have been reared in a household where cuddles and good food are considered important, and that they have good character genes to pass on to their offspring.

If you are lucky, the cats you have marked out at a cat show will also be the ones the judges like. The parents of your kitten queen-to-be may be top show winners with great personalities, splendid condition and a helpful breeder/owner.

HOME CHARMS

Before you commit yourself, visit the mother of your queen-to-be in its home, as this is very different from seeing her in the restricted atmosphere of a show. If other cats are there, such as her parents or siblings, you will be able to see how they interact with each other. These are the blood relations of your breeding queen.

Ask detailed questions about their pedigrees and breeding records. It is far better, for example, to acquire a female for breeding which comes from a long line of successful mothers that rear strong litters with no fatalities, than to go for a line of top-winning cats with only a marginally successful breeding record. Responsible breeders will also be assessing you as a future

◆ RIGHT
A Siamese demonstrates how to be a good mother. When you are choosing a kitten to found your breeding line, it is important to look at her mother, and how she reacts with her offspring. Good relationships can have a knock-on effect through the generations.

breeder in your own right, and note how their cats respond to you. Before releasing a kitten, they may even ask for references from your vet.

COMING HOME

Finally, you have the new kitten; you have joined the breed club. The period between now and when she is ready for her first mating is a key preparation time. Your queen-to-be must have the best possible diet as recommended by her breeder. She must be played with and exercised until her muscular condition is superb, and generally handled with love and tenderness so that she bonds with you. When the time comes for her to have her kittens, she will then do so in the confident knowledge of the support of her owners.

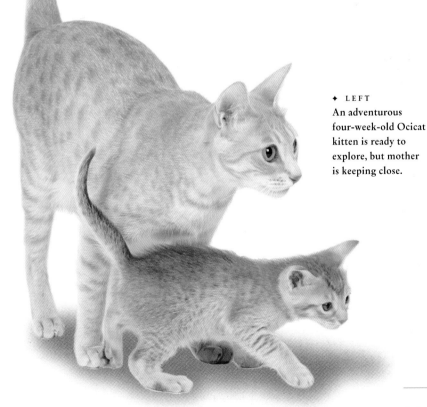

◆ LEFT
An adventurous four-week-old Ocicat kitten is ready to explore, but mother is keeping close.

READY FOR MATING?

It is quite obvious when a female is ready for mating. She starts what is known as "calling" – although this can be more like shrieking or wailing in some breeds, such as Siamese. Some Persians content themselves with dainty little mews and miaows. The female displays some brazen behaviour, rolling and dragging herself around the floor, flicking her tail and raising her rump to expose the slightly reddened area beneath. She may also lose interest in her food. If her behaviour fools you into thinking she is unwell, try picking her up by her neck folds (as an interested tom would do) and stroke along her back. If she responds with pleasure, pads her feet and raises her tail, she is definitely in season.

The average age of sexual maturity in a female is around six months, but cats of oriental origin such as Siamese and Burmese can be as early as fourteen or sixteen weeks. British Shorthairs and Persians do not start calling much before ten months. Generally, tom cats become sexually mature a month or two later than females of the same breed. The time of year also has an

◆ ABOVE

A Siamese female in season rolls around and thrashes her tail. Siamese are notorious for announcing their sexual readiness with loud and strident calling.

◆ BELOW

A Bi-colour Seal Point Ragdoll tom has taken a fancy to a Ragdoll and Turkish Van cross. If they mate successfully, their kittens will be very pretty, but they will not be pedigreed stock.

◆ **BELOW**
When selecting a stud, always look for the best example. While this Red Persian is a little out of coat, his type is superb, and he will no doubt father excellent kittens.

effect on the first call. If due in autumn or winter, it may be delayed until the warmer months of spring.

The cycle is approximately 21 days and females may come into oestrus (on call) for about three to ten days. They continue to be fertile until at least fourteen years of age.

It is best to let the young queen run through the first couple of cycles – until she is at least a year old – rather than put her to stud immediately. This gets the system going and reduces the risk of problems at birth.

CHOOSING THE MALE

Many breed clubs publish a stud list of proven males, but the breeder from whom you bought the female is likely to know of suitable mates. An experienced breeder is also likely to know about genetically compatible lines, and even if you have some ideas of your own, it is important to take expert advice.

If you go to a show to look for potential partners, do not be tempted to go for the stunning new male Grand Champion. Other breeders may be clamouring to use him, but the wiser choice would be his father. Not only has he proved himself to be the sire of outstanding stock, but with a maiden queen it is wiser to use an experienced stud for the first mating.

RENDEZVOUS

Before committing yourself to a particular stud, visit the breeder to check the conditions in which the maiden queen is to be kept. This is an opportunity also to ask vital questions about the number and the supervision of matings. Documentation on the participating animals that needs to be exchanged varies according to the conditions for entry to stud, but for your female include the following:

◆ pedigree
◆ registration and/or transfer
◆ up-to-date vaccination certificate
◆ current test certificates showing negative status for both feline infectious leukaemia and feline immunodeficiency virus (FIV).

The stud owner may require the tests to have been carried out within the last 24 hours, although others accept tests within the past five to seven days. The conditions and fees should be agreed before taking the queen to the stud. Conditions of the mating might include an agreement that no males from a resulting litter will be used for breeding, or for the pick of the litter to be substituted in lieu of a mating fee. It is usual for there to be another free mating should the queen fail to become pregnant.

On a more informal level, the stud owner should want to know the pet name of the cat and the diet she is used to.

◆ **LEFT**
Whatever the breed, it is important that the male is neither monorchid (one testicled) nor cryptorchid (hidden testicled): this Korat is fully endowed!

◆ **BELOW**
The ideal Tabby stud should not only be of first-class type, but have clear, well-defined markings.

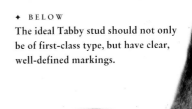

THE MATING

When the young queen starts to call, contact the stud owner. Both animals must be in good health, and have their nails clipped beforehand.

The journey to the stud usually takes place on the second or third day of the call. The stud's owner prepares for the arrival of the queen by thoroughly disinfecting the entire stud run and the queen's quarters. The queen is settled in her quarters within the stud run, where the stud can "talk" to her. This enables the queen to become accustomed to the stud's presence, and prepares her for mating.

At a quiet moment, the stud's owner releases the queen from her quarters. If all goes to plan, she crouches ready to receive the male; he grasps her by the scruff with his teeth, and taps her rump with one of his back legs until she raises it and flicks her tail over. The first entry of the male induces ovulation in the female and may result in fertilization, though subsequent matings are more likely to do so. (Note that your queen is likely to remain fertile for several days, so keep her in when she returns home.)

When sexual climax is reached, the female utters a strange cry that is only ever heard at this time. As soon as he withdraws from the female, the male moves away as the female turns on him with tooth and claw. She then rolls around, washing furiously for a couple of minutes. Only after she has done this is she calm again. Several matings need to take place over two or three days to try to ensure that the female becomes pregnant.

The stud owner supervises matings so that no harm comes to either stud or queen, but, in many cases, the male and female soon develop a bond. They are then allowed to run together and mating can take place freely. It is very common for the queen to take over the stud's bed and to assume matriarchal dominance. At the end of her stay, the stud owner will provide a certificate giving details of:

- ✦ the stud's pedigree
  - ✦ number of matings observed
    - ✦ dates of matings
    - ✦ expected date of litter arrival
    - ✦ the agreed stud fee and conditions

✦ BELOW
The queen and tom go through preparatory rituals before mating takes place, but once the male has ejaculated, he moves out of the way to avoid a sharp cuff from his partner.

✦ TOP
A female does not ovulate (release her eggs) until the moment of mating. One of the triggers is the male taking hold of the queen's neck fur; this also has the practical effect of keeping her in one place.

◆ BELOW
Towards the end of a pregnancy, most cats
require more rest than usual, and this Persian is
relaxing before her confinement.

THE PREGNANCY

The average gestation period for cats is
between 63 and 68 days. Occasionally,
healthy kittens are produced even at
61 days. Kittens produced at or before
this time usually require very
specialized nursing, as key systems
have not fully developed. Some
females carry their kittens for as long
as 70 days. In this event, the kittens
may be larger than normal.

SIGNS OF PREGNANCY

The first indication that a cat is
pregnant (or in kitten) is when she
does not come on heat two or three
weeks after mating. Soon after this,
there will be visible signs of
pregnancy: the nipples become rather
swollen and take on a deep coral-pink
tone, a process that is called pinking
up. Very experienced breeders may
know a cat is in kitten a few days in
advance of this, as there is sometimes a
ridging of the muscles of the cat's
stomach. A vet is able to confirm a
pregnancy by feeling the cat's
abdomen after three or four weeks.

ANTENATAL CARE

A pregnant cat should be encouraged
to maintain a normal lifestyle. You
can increase the amount of food you
give her from about the fifth week of
pregnancy, and introduce a vitamin
supplement. In a feral state, a cat
gorges itself as it does not know where
the next meal is coming from. Your
cat will let you know how much food
she wants. Seek veterinary advice if
you are in any doubt.

Climbing, jumping, running – and
hunting if the cat is free-range – are all
normal physical activities, even for a
pregnant pedigree. Do remember,
however, that allowing a pregnant
female free range may expose her to
other dangers. She may slow down a
bit towards the end of her term, but
activity ensures that good, strong
muscle tone is maintained. This is
essential for a natural, successful birth.

After about four weeks, the queen's
stomach starts to distend, the nipples
become very prominent, and she
begins to look pregnant. By around
28 days, all the kittens' internal organs
have formed, and the embryos are
about 2.5cm (1in) long. The skeleton
develops from about 40 days, and at
50 days, the kittens quicken – show
signs of movement. Look for rippling,
sliding motions along the mother's
flank; they are most noticeable when
she is resting.

About a week before the birth, the
queen starts looking for a nesting
place. It is a good idea to prepare a
cardboard-box house for the queen
with lots of plain paper inside for her
to tear up. If this is not done, she will
do her best to get into wardrobes
(closets), drawers, airing cupboards –
anywhere warm and draught-free.

◆ LEFT
Given a choice,
your queen would
probably nest in a
most inconvenient
spot. A kittening box
is ideal for both
mother and owner,
but do make sure the
cat is used to and
comfortable with
both the box and its
location well before
the birth.

THE KITTENING

Birth is an exciting but messy business, which is why there should be a lot of padding in the kittening box and the area beneath and around the box should be easy to clean and disinfect without disturbing the inmates too much.

About 24 hours before the actual birth, the queen enters the first stage of labour. Outward physical signs are very few. There may be the odd faint ripple along the flank of the cat, and experienced breeders will note that her breathing through the nose has become shallow and rapid on occasion. Close examination reveals a flickering of the nostrils during these early, very faint contractions. Towards the end of this process, a small mucous plug may be found in the bedding, or adhering to the hair close to the cat's vulva.

The next stage can take quite a long time, depending on the number of kittens. It is important not to panic: as long as the queen shows no signs of physical distress, all is going well. During this second stage, the classic signs of major contractions are clearly visible. The queen is breathing deeply and her whole abdomen seems to shudder and ripple downwards.

Eventually, a membrane sac containing a kitten and fluid starts to emerge from the queen's vulva and it may be possible to see the kitten's head within the sac. Sometimes the sac will burst at this point when it is said

+ ABOVE LEFT
A newborn kitten has just emerged and broken free from the protective sac of amniotic fluid.

+ ABOVE RIGHT
Mother's first task is to take her newborn kitten and wash it thoroughly, especially around the nose and mouth to clear respiratory passages so that it can breathe – and utter its first cries.

MIDWIFE EQUIPMENT

+ disinfected, blunt-ended scissors
+ sterile surgical gloves
+ kitchen towels
+ hot water
+ ordinary towels
+ towelling face cloths
+ water-based lubricant

that the waters have broken. Often, the birth is so rapid that the kitten is born before the sac bursts.

The queen clears the sac from around the kitten and immediately washes the newborn, particularly around the nose and mouth. This prompts the kitten to get rid of any amniotic residue from its respiratory system and it will often begin to cry. By this time secondary contractions have expelled the placenta (afterbirth), which the queen will instinctively eat. In a feral state, this would provide her with food and nutrients during the first couple of days after kittening when she needs to recover. Hormones in the placenta promote milk secretion, and also help the uterus to contract, preventing a haemorrhage, which is a normal occurence after every birth. In the wild, such haemorrhaging could lead a predator to the kittens' nest. The queen also chews through the umbilical cord. In a straightforward birth, the queen, even a maiden queen,

+ LEFT
One week old, blind, deaf, hungry – and not at all domesticated.

◆ BELOW
A non-pedigreed litter has settled down after the trials of birth.

will usually cope with everything. However, it may be that you will have to assist on occasions. For this, a range of equipment should be within easy reach.

BREECH BIRTH

It is normal for some kittens to be born backwards, with hind feet being presented first. If the rump and tail rather than the stretched-out hind feet are presented first, this is a breech birth and can be a problem. It is so easy to become impatient and want to get your hands in the nest to help out, but the real need to do this should be very carefully weighed up.

If the queen is contracting strongly, it is likely that she will be able to birth the kitten quite normally. This way round is just a little more difficult, as the head is not widening the birth passage so that the rest of the body can slide through. However, if the waters have burst and the kitten is taking a very long time to be born, there is a risk of brain damage or still-birth and the kitten should be helped out as quickly as possible.

If the legs are coming first, quickly slip on the surgical gloves and smear a little of the lubrication around the vulva. Never pull on any part of the kitten – it is an extremely delicate

organism capable of being very easily damaged. As the queen's contractions push the legs further out of the vulva, use index and middle finger to "scissor" the legs right next to the opening of the vulva. As the contractions cease, the natural effect is for the legs to be drawn back into the vulva. The breeder's fingers will hold the legs in position until the next set of contractions. Then as more of the legs appear, use the index and middle fingers of the other hand to

repeat the process. Generally, once the hips have emerged, the queen can do the rest by herself.

In the case of a rump or tail breech birth, you may need to gently insert a lubricated finger beside the kitten and hold it as a hook. But it must be emphasized that, in most cases, the queen knows what is best and can manage by herself.

APPARENT STILL-BIRTH

Sometimes a kitten will be born apparently lifeless. This may not be the case; it may not be breathing and be in a state of shock. If the queen does not immediately rasp away at the kitten's face, it is your job to do it. To clear any excess fluid from the nose and lungs, hold the kitten in your hand with index finger going over and supporting its head. Gently swing the kitten downwards two or three times and then wipe and stimulate the face

◆ BELOW
The mother and her kittens need to be watched
carefully at first, in case any complications arise.
However, usually the mother is quite capable of
looking after and training her kittens on her own.

around the nose and nostrils. At the same time, rub its little body vigorously. In most cases this will get it going but you may have to resort to mouth-to-mouth resuscitation.

It may be that the kitten has suffered some form of foetal distress during the birth process and has, in fact, died. The cause may be more serious, and a dead kitten should be laid aside carefully for a post-mortem examination to establish the cause.

QUEEN DISTRESS
Even very experienced queens may become distressed and unable to birth their kittens. Because of this possibility it is wise to let your veterinarian know when the kittens are due. The most common form of distress is the lack of strong contractions. The vet may inject the queen with oxytocin, a hormone to improve contractions. If this does not work, birth by Caesarean section may be the only option. This is done very rapidly and with the minimum amount of anaesthetic, so that the queen is well able to look after her kittens.

One of the reasons why it is essential to examine the breeding record of the bloodline from which a queen is obtained is to check for any predisposition to the need for Caesarean sections.

POST-NATAL CARE
While it is rare for a healthy queen to encounter problems after pregnancy, a close watch should always be kept for the following conditions:

◆ Pyometra: an infection of the uterus characterized by a thick, off-white discharge. This condition is not serious if caught quickly and treated with antibiotics. In a serious form it will mean that the queen will have to be spayed.

◆ Eclampsia (milk fever): caused by a dramatic fall in calcium levels in the queen who will begin to convulse. An immediate intra-muscular or intravenous injection of calcium from the vet brings immediate recovery.

◆ Mastitis: the queen's mammary glands become hard, lumpy and hot due to an infection. Treatment is with antibiotics. Temporary relief can be given by the use of warm compresses on the affected area.

◆ Lack of milk: the queen's milk can dry up if she doesn't have sufficient wholesome food and drink; or the kittens are not suckling vigorously enough; or through mastitis. A homeopathic remedy such as Lachesis or hormone treatment may result in a return of the milk supply. If not, the kittens may have to be hand-fed until they are weaned. This means two-hourly feeds with a commercially available substitute milk. The vet may know of breeders who are specialists in the techniques of hand-feeding.

ABNORMALITIES
Defects are rare. They include:
◆ cleft palate or hare-lip
◆ lack of eyes
◆ heart defects including hole in the heart
◆ umbilical hernia
◆ intestines on the outside

GROWING UP

If the litter is strong and healthy, the queen will require no assistance from you for the first two to three weeks. However, do change the bedding regularly (provided this does not upset the mother) and make sure the mother has plenty to eat: she may need three times as much as usual. The kittens' eyes open at around a week old and they will stop hissing at you every time you pick them up.

It is important to handle the kittens from the start. Encourage them to become used to the human voice and contact by picking them up and stroking them gently and regularly, and crooning to them. Experts used to advise that queens and their newborn kittens should be kept in a warm, dark, secluded place. However, this is just about the best way to make kittens nervous of people and activity. Once the kittens are weaned they can be introduced into the wider home environment and visitors, even if this is from within the sanctuary of a kitten pen. Social contact increases their confidence to tackle new situations when they leave home at twelve to sixteen weeks of age.

EATING HABITS

The mother guides her kittens to her teats. They knead the teats with their paws and then start to suckle. The colostrum milk of the first few days is rich in the mother's antibodies and nutrients which protect the newborn kittens from infection. The kittens should be gradually weaned off their mother's milk. There is no specific time when this starts to happen, though they may begin to eat their mother's food at three to four weeks. It is not unusual for a kitten to remain

◆ BELOW
Seven weeks old: these three look harmless enough, but at this age they will be learning to hunt and fend for themselves through play.

on mother's milk for the first five weeks. Kittens must be fully weaned by 12 weeks, when they are ready to go to a new owner. They are actually capable of lapping water and of being on a solid diet by about six weeks.

The first solid food should be high-quality canned kitten food, finely

◆ BELOW
Nine weeks old: active, strong and independent enough to venture outside – but not until it has had its first vaccinations.

minced cooked meat or poultry, or flaked white fish. Variety will encourage broad taste and good habits in later life as well as a balanced diet. Avoid dried food at this stage, and feed the kittens small quantities four to six times daily at three to four weeks of age, gradually reducing to three or four times daily from then on.

Until they begin eating solid foods, the kittens do not need to use the litter tray (pan). The mother cleans them herself. You may find that the kittens simply copy their mother and use the tray

◆ LEFT
A Siamese mother shows her kitten exactly where, when and how to use the litter tray (pan). It is unlikely that the kitten will need any extra training from its owner.

◆ BELOW
Some are more interested than others in the prospect of solid food. One of these Siamese kittens may be reflecting on the warmth and comfort of its mother's breast.

without any help from you. If not, you can try placing the kittens in the tray immediately after each feed. The tray should be in a quiet spot where the floor and surroundings can be easily cleaned and disinfected. From this moment until the kittens leave to go to their new homes, your

management of the environment is extremely important. Where there is a lack of hygiene, there is a risk of disease and infection. The kittens may also form bad habits which they will carry with them to a new home. Such a situation would be a poor advertisement for a breeder.

THE BASICS OF INHERITANCE

Before you begin to breed from your cat, it is important to investigate her genetic inheritance and that of the stud you are mating her with. She is the product of a vast number of generations of maybe 50 or more years of recorded breeding. A catalogue of cat show successes may also indicate a healthy genetic coding that she will pass on to her offspring. You can discover just how she acquired her particular colouring and characteristics, and work out what her kittens are likely to have.

Quite how characteristics such as colour or pattern passed from one generation of cats to another was not

◆ LEFT
In an attempt to breed out blue eyes in white cats, which seemed to coincide with a tendency to deafness, white cats were cross-bred with orange-eyed breeds. Sometimes the result was an eye of each colour – which became a variety in its own right.

◆ BELOW
The blue colouring in a proud father – a Persian Blue Bi-colour – has diluted to lilac in his kitten.

understood until the second half of the 1800s. An Austrian monk called Gregor Mendel began to unlock the secrets of heredity and genetics in the 1850s, which made programmed breeding possible for the first time. Instead of random experimentation, breeders could select and cross-mate cats with the characteristics they wanted to promote and be passed on to the offspring.

THE POWER OF THE GENE

The instrument of inheritance which controls particular features or behavioural traits is the gene. Genes are responsible for all inherited characteristics, from coat colour and pattern, length of tail or shape of ears, to health and character. A kitten inherits half of its genes from its mother and half from its father. The arrangement of genes is different for each kitten in a litter, so each one is genetically unique.

There are certain genes carrying specific characteristics, such as the red gene, that can only be passed down through the generations by either a male or a female, but not both. These sex-linked genes are the reason why, for example, tortoiseshells are

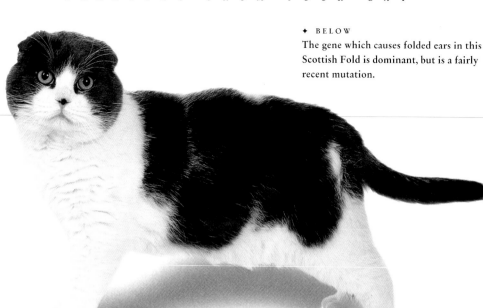

✦ BELOW
The gene which causes folded ears in this Scottish Fold is dominant, but is a fairly recent mutation.

patterns such as blue or self. That is why two black parents may produce a blue or chocolate kitten and why two tabby parents may produce a Self kitten.

Sometimes the fundamental character of a gene is altered by an outside factor, such as radiation or other environmental situations. Japanese Bobtails and Manx cats both developed in isolated island communities which meant that they were forced to interbreed. A mutation gene occurred that resulted in the lack of a tail – which is, in fact, a malformation of the spine similar to spina bifida in humans. Some breeders have taken advantage of such mutations and developed new breeds from them.

always female. A normal male cat cannot inherit both the red and the "not red" gene.

Some genes are more powerful than others and are called dominant genes. If one dominant colour gene and one recessive colour gene occur in a newly fertilized egg, the dominant gene determines the colour of the kitten. The recessive gene, however, could be passed on through several generations without coming out, or being expressed. Then, if it met up with a matching recessive gene, from the other parent, its particular gene characteristic would be expressed. What this means in cat terms is that there are certain dominant colour or pattern genes such as black or tabby, that override recessive colours and

✦ ABOVE
Polydactylism (excess number of toes) in this cream kitten is caused by a dominant gene. It is not permitted in any pedigree breeds.

✦ RIGHT
Natural mutation has taken place in Manx breeds, probably as a result of enforced interbreeding on an island – in this case, the Isle of Man off the west coast of England.

THE ART OF SELECTION

◆ LEFT
Cinnamon is a recessive gene to black and is carried on the same gene locus as chocolate.

The colour range in a litter is determined by genes inherited from the parents, and whether those genes are dominant or recessive. Each kitten will inherit genes from both parents, but in a unique combination.

Genes are found in pairs. Black is dominant to chocolate and cinnamon, so a cat with one black gene will be black, whereas if it has no black genes it will be chocolate or cinnamon. Within this same pair, chocolate is dominant to cinnamon, so a cinnamon cat must have two cinnamon genes (a cat with one gene for chocolate and one for cinnamon will be chocolate in colour). The dilute gene, which dilutes the pigment of a cat from black to blue, chocolate to lilac, cinnamon to fawn, or red to cream, is recessive. In order for a cat to be a dilute colour it must have two dilute genes.

A tabby pattern is carried by the agouti gene which gives each hair a dark tip and alternate bands of light and dark colour. A non-agouti gene blocks the production of the light band in each hair, so producing a solid-coloured coat. White fur is the product of a gene which carries no pigmentation at all.

◆ ABOVE RIGHT
The lineage of this Blue Abyssinian would have included two dilute recessive genes and a black gene.

◆ RIGHT
This Exotic Shorthair must be female as she is a tortoiseshell – a colour produced by the presence of one red and one 'not red' gene.

COLOUR MUTATIONS

Black The first colour recessive mutation from the ancestral grey/brown agouti. Produces an extremely dark, solid colour perceived as black

Chocolate Recessive gene to black creating a dark brown

Cinnamon Recessive gene to black and chocolate. Carried on the same gene locus as chocolate, producing a light-brown colour with a warm (almost red-tinted) tone

Orange Sex-linked gene (carried on the X chromosome, so females XX can have two such genes, males XY can have only one).This alters black, chocolate and cinnamon to an orange (red, auburn, ginger) colour. Females are not sterile

Dilution Very often known as the "blue" gene as the presence of the recessive dilution with black creates a grey (lavender-blue) individual. Also affects other colours. Alters the structure of the pigment cells

Dilution + black = blue
Dilution + chocolate = lilac
Dilution + cinnamon = fawn
Dilution + orange = cream

Tortoiseshell The presence of the orange gene plus black and its recessive colours of chocolate and cinnamon creates the two-coloured tortoiseshell female, i.e. black, chocolate and cinnamon tortoiseshells. In combination with the dilution gene the pastel blue-cream, lilac-cream and fawn-cream are created. The rare occurrence of the tortoiseshell male is probably due to the presence of an extra X chromosome. The males are usually sterile

Inhibitor Dominant and, as its name suggests, inhibiting – this gene reduces ground colour, e.g. the rufous colour of the brown tabby to the pewter ground of the silver tabby, or converting a self cat to a smoke

Dilute modifier Dominant gene, the presence of which is still disputed. Creates a rather dull brownish-grey colour known as caramel. It has no effect on the dominant colours black, chocolate, cinnamon or red. Probably originated in Chinchilla Persian stock and is to be found in several breeds of pedigreed cat

Full colour and its recessives Recessives to full colour are Burmese, Siamese, and blue-eyed and pink-eyed Albinos.

Burmese affects black, reducing it to a lustrous brown, or sable.

In the Siamese cat, black becomes a warm-toned seal.

Albinos are almost completely lacking in pigmentation (the blue-eyed version) or entirely without pigmentation (the pink-eyed version). Both may be completely or incompletely light-sensitive. Extremely rare in cats, although a race of Albino Siamese was discovered in America

PATTERN MUTATIONS

Agouti The dominant ancestral pattern of the domestic cat in which the individual hairs of the coat are banded with colour. Normally light or grey at the roots of the hair with the darkest colour at the tip

Tabby A range of pattern genes which is not seen unless in conjunction with the agouti gene or the orange gene:

The mackerel tabby has thinly striped markings like those along the sides of the mackerel fish.

The spotted tabby, in which the thin lines are broken down into clearly defined spots, may be a recessive to the mackerel tabby or created as the result of the effects of polygenes.

Abyssinian or ticked tabby markings are reduced almost entirely or restricted to face, legs and tail. This is the dominant pattern.

Blotched, marble or classic tabby markings include a bulls-eye on each flank and further marbling of colour on an agouti-based ground colour. The gene causing this is recessive to the other forms of tabby marking

Tipping or shading It seems likely that the fairly recently discovered wide band gene combined with the agouti gene, affects the degree of colour shown towards the tip of each hair. The effect of the gene varies from the lightest of tipping, as seen in the chinchilla, to quite heavy shading, where as much as half the hair may be dark. This effect may be mimicked by a very heavily silvered smoke, although never to the lightness seen in the chinchilla. The presence of the wide band gene appears to be confirmed by the existence of the golden chinchilla or shaded cat, which is rufous with dark tips to the hair. The ground colour has not been inhibited

White Dominant gene which covers all other colours in an "overcoat" effect to create an all-white coat. In its pure form, in which all offspring produced are white, blue-eyed or odd-eyed cats may well suffer from hearing loss, either partial or total. This is less likely to happen where one parent is white and the other coloured

White spotting A dominant gene that results in areas of colour being suppressed by areas of white, creating the bi- or tri-coloured cat. White spotting can range from a few white hairs creating a chest mark or a spot on the belly, to an almost complete absence of colour. The van pattern suppresses colour to form flashes on the head and a solid-coloured tail, whereas the harlequin shows a more spotted pattern of colour on the body and legs as well

Himalayan or Siamese A recessive gene in which the colour is restricted to the "points" of the cat, these being the face (mask), legs and tail. This pattern is usually associated with intense blue eyes

Burmese A recessive gene to full colour, but incompletely dominant to Siamese. The body appears to be a solid colour, though of reduced intensity

Tonkinese A slightly pointed hybrid pattern created by a cross between Burmese and Siamese cats

✦ RIGHT
An Oriental Classic Tabby has tabby markings on an agouti background.

✦ ABOVE
Maine Coon Black Smoke. This colour is produced by a combination of self black plus the inhibitor gene, giving a silver undercoat.

✦ RIGHT
A Siamese Blue Point has one black, two dilute and two Siamese genes. Selective breeding has reduced the incidence of squints and kinks in Siamese tails.

◆ BELOW
The recessive gene for hairlessness has been discovered and lost many times. When a hairless kitten was born in Canada, in 1966, breeders started to develop the breed known as Sphynx.

◆ BELOW
A longhaired coat needs two recessive genes for long hair, but in Persians generations of selective breeding have lengthened the coat of the non-pedigreed longhair to the magnificent coat seen here.

◆ RIGHT
A strange, curly kitten from Oregon proved, on first mating, to have a previously unknown dominant gene which gave it and its kittens curly hair.

COAT QUALITY AND LENGTH

Shorthair Dominant gene restricting coat length. Strong guardhairs give impression of a crispness or sleekness of texture

Semi-longhair Recessive gene basically producing a long-coated cat but with more noticeable length on neck, chest, rear legs and tail. Coat generally self-maintaining

Longhair Produced by the same recessive gene as the semi-longhair, but bred to produce a coat of extreme length, softness/silkiness of texture and requiring much human intervention to maintain it

Wirehair Dominant gene producing crimped, wiry, upstanding coat

Rexed coat Recessive group of genes, not always genetically compatible, producing a mostly tightly curled, soft-textured coat

Selkirk Rex coat Dominant gene which is the exception to the general Rex group, producing a shaggy, plush-coated cat

Sphynx Recessive gene officially designated hairless but, in fact, producing a peach-skin-like coat which is quite different in quality from the truly hairless individuals still sometimes produced in Devon Rex cats. A hairless cat produced by a dominant gene is seen in Russia

Showing Your Cat

A cat has no particular interest in whether it goes to a show or not, but its owner can gain a great deal of satisfaction from having a prize-winning animal and become part of the sociable cat-showing circuit. Shows provide an arena for the serious cat breeder or committed owner of pedigreed animals to display their stock. However, there are often more relaxed classes for ordinary household pets as well.

◆ FACING PAGE
A winner of several Best in Show awards, a Supreme Grand Premier sits with its rosettes and prizes. The kudos for the owner exceeds any real financial gain.

◆ ABOVE
A Persian's coat is carefully groomed before a show.

THE REWARDS OF SHOWING

Showing your cat is an expensive business, even if the animal has championship potential. The rewards are likely to be pride in your – and your cat's – achievements, a rosette and perhaps a silver cup or a supply of commercial cat food rather than prize money. Apart from the cost and maintenance of your pedigreed cat, there are equipment and travelling costs as well as high entry fees to consider. However, for the committed cat fancier – the person who is interested in breeding and showing pedigree cats – there are many other rewards. Cat shows present the ideal opportunity to find out about the various breeds. You can make valuable contacts with breeders and look out for your next new kitten, or for suitable mates for your queen. You will become part of the cat fanciers' network, check out the latest breeds and commercial cat products, make friends and fill in your social calendar with cat-related events. Whether your

♦ LEFT
♦ LEFT
A White Persian at an American cat show sits with its rosettes in a decorated pen.

♦ BELOW LEFT
Cat shows provide an opportunity for like-minded people to compare notes and make friends.

♦ ABOVE
The whole family can be involved – and may prevent the cat from becoming too bored.

♦ LEFT
It may be very boring and rather noisy to sit in a small pen at a cat show all day, but the impressive display of rosettes suggest that this cat is worth breeding from.

cat actively enjoys the show or not is debatable. Most cats are so adaptable they will tolerate being confined to a pen for the best part of a day. Others may have a shy or timid nature, or may be particularly active; in either case it would not be fair to subject them to the show scene. If you introduce a kitten to showing at an early age, it is more likely to adapt. Some cats even appear to relish the attention and admiration from passers-by. If you are taking a cat to its first show, keep a close eye on it; if it is unhappy, it will let you know.

QUALITY CONTROL

It is through being judged at shows that new breeds gain acceptance and established breeds keep up to scratch. If a new breed does not make it through the various levels of judging, from local show to national championship, it is unlikely to survive. When judges study a cat, they are making sure that it conforms with the standards set for that breed. If they spot signs of, say, an aggressive temperament, or a deformity in an up-and-coming breed, they can disqualify the cat and stipulate that it should not be used for breeding.

A NEW CRAZE FOR CATS

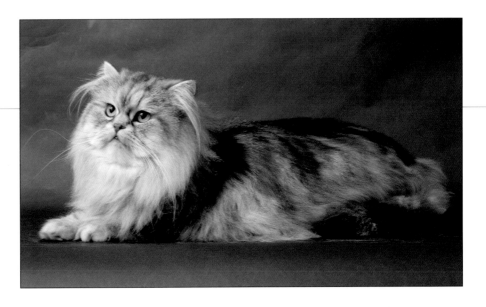

A growing interest in the selective breeding of pedigreed animals and the arrival of exotic cats such as Persians and Turkish Angoras in the West led to the first official cat show in London in 1871. There is a record of a show being held in Winchester, England in 1598, but the London event had the cats in show pens, 25 classes for different breeds, and judging benches. Domestic shorthairs and Persians dominated the early shows, although there were some foreign introductions. The first benched cat show in America was held at Madison Square Garden, New York in 1895, in which Maine Coon Cats featured strongly.

These early events spawned a whole new leisure activity, and the breeding and showing bug soon spread to most parts of the world. Today, scarcely a day, and certainly not a weekend, goes by without a cat show being held somewhere, whether it is organized by a breed club for their specific breed, or for all breeds at local, as well as area and national levels.

THE ORGANIZERS

Throughout the world, organizations register pedigrees and stipulate rules for running shows. Individual breed clubs and area clubs are affiliated to one or other of these authorities.

In the United Kingdom, the Governing Council of the Cat Fancy (GCCF), formed in 1910, is the main regulatory body. The Governing Council of the Cat Fancy in Ireland (GCCFI) licenses shows in the same way as the GCCF, although it is not affiliated to it, and has a close liaison with the GCCF. The Cat Association of Britain (CA), formed in the early

1980s, also registers pedigree cats; it is affiliated to the European *Fédération Internationale Féline* (Fifé) and runs shows under European rules.

Fifé, founded in 1949, is not just a European organization, but has member countries throughout the world (though not the major cat-fancying countries of the United States and Canada, Australia and New Zealand or Japan). The many independent clubs in Europe work as autonomous federations with their own registries, but many liaise with each other. Recently, more shows have been judged by both Fifé and independent judges. Organizational

problems are shared, and judges from both systems can meet and discuss ideas and standards.

In the United States, the largest nationwide registering bodies are the Cat Fanciers' Association (CFA) and The International Cat Association (TICA), although there are many other organizations spread the length and breadth of North America. Some of them are regionally based, such as the American Cat Association (ACA) in California.

Your first step in showing is to contact your area or national organization for their schedule of shows, and show rules.

✦ ABOVE
The early cat shows at the end of the 1800s were dominated by Persians and domestic shorthairs in the United Kingdom.

✦ LEFT
Now all that prodding and poking is over, and the rosettes are up, maybe a chap can have a nap.

ENTERING A SHOW

First go to a show without your cat; it will be much easier if you have a clear idea of noise level, numbers, conditions and how the events are run.

The organizing bodies usually publish an annual list of the shows under their jurisdiction, which you can buy for a small fee. These publications should have the name and address of a contact for each show to whom you can then apply for a schedule – allow about three months before the event. The schedule contains the rules under which the show is operating, the classes that can be entered, and qualification requirements for each. It is essential to read the rules carefully and go through the relevant class details before you proceed any further. You also need to check in your rules for such qualifications as the lowest age of entry for a kitten (usually fourteen weeks), at what stage your animal should join an adult class (usually nine months), and what the restrictions are for neutered and

◆ BELOW
Grooming does not just take place on the day of a show; the health and maintenance programme has to start weeks before to ensure the cat is in peak condition, even if it is a non-pedigree.

entire animals. Any household pets over the age of nine months, for example, must be neutered.

There will also be an entry form with instructions on how to complete it, as well as details of the entry fees charged and how to pay them. Read it all meticulously. If you get something wrong, you could be refused entry on the day. If you are uncertain about any aspect, contact the show management.

If you are showing a pedigreed cat, you will need to refer to its registration

◆ BELOW
Some all-breed shows are enormous events with up to 1,500 entrants and thousands of visitors. This is the National Cat Club Show in Britain.

CAT KIT FOR A SHOW

- ◆ Vaccination certificates
- ◆ Grooming equipment
- ◆ Blanket (white, if UK show)
- ◆ Food and water bowls (white, if UK show)
- ◆ Food and water (for the cat)
- ◆ Litter tray/pan (white, if UK show)
- ◆ Litter
- ◆ White ribbon (for the identification label)
- ◆ Cleaning materials
- ◆ Disinfectant (suitable to clean the cat's pen)
- ◆ String and scissors (to secure pen if necessary)
- ◆ Toy
- ◆ Decorations on a theme (if appropriate)

details (obtained from the original breeder), and know its breed number, date of birth, parentage and breeder. Your breeder may be able to advise on which classes to enter if you are unsure.

PREPARING FOR A SHOW
Preparing your cat for a show will take more than just a quick comb through. Longhaired varieties need to be bathed and groomed intensively for weeks preceding the show. Even shorthaired cats need in-depth preparation to ensure that they look and feel perfect to the touch.

On the day of the show, make sure you have all the equipment you will need neatly assembled – keep it all together in a cat bag – and leave in good time. Many European shows last two days, the panel of judges taking different classes on each day. American and Canadian shows may even extend to three days, and therefore need a great deal of careful extra thought and preparation.

WHAT HAPPENS AT A SHOW?

◆ BELOW
A vet assists in checking for any structural defects at a national cat show.

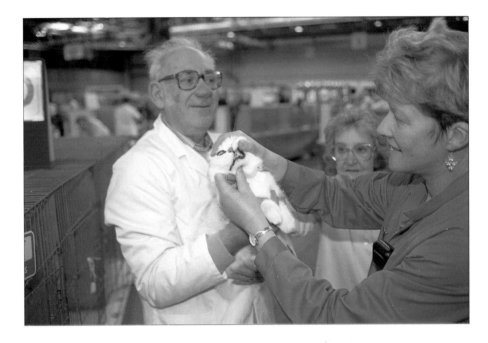

Show style and rules vary from country to country, and according to the size of the show. Individual breed clubs organize their own events, which tend to be small-scale, informal, friendly occasions. Others may be organized by major registering bodies, or may be compound affairs, with a number of separate shows running concurrently for different breeds or classes, each one presided over by a separate judge or team of judges.

Three months before the show date, send off your entry form and fee. When you receive confirmation, and possibly a copy of your cat's entry in the show catalogue, check this as soon as possible. If there is anything wrong, however small, inform the organizer who will check the details against the initial entry form. If you have made a major mistake in your application, you run the risk of disqualification unless the official catalogue is corrected.

When you arrive with your cat at a European show, including all British shows, you will probably have to queue so that your cat can be checked by a vet (vetted-in); in some countries it is left to trust that your cat is in good health and has all the necessary inoculations. For vetting-in you need to have the cat's up-to-date certificates of vaccination ready, as the vet will want to see them. Just before your turn with the vet, a show official will give you a pen number, an identification label to attach to the cat, a veterinary pass card and a check card for the classes entered, with which you claim rosettes or prize money later on. However, if the vaccination certificates are not in order, or there is any suspicion of parasitic infestation, or anything else is wrong, the vet will

not allow the cat in. Once through the vetting-in, find the allocated pen. This is where the cat will stay for the duration of the show, apart from when it is taken out to be judged.

LAST-MINUTE ATTENTION

When you find your allotted pen, it is a good idea to clean it with the cat-compatible disinfectant you have brought with you. Check the security on the cage and make sure there are no

loose or jagged ends. Attach the identification label (known as a tally) to some thin ribbon or shirring elastic and tie it loosely round the cat's neck. If it objects, as it almost certainly will, do not insist, especially if the cat is in a pen by itself; tie the label to the outside of the cage.

Setting the cat in the cage is termed benching, and all the information you need about this is in the show rules, including what you can and cannot put

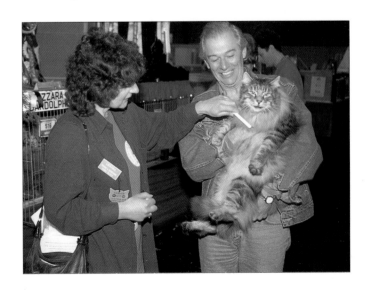

◆ LEFT
There may be time for a last-minute groom before the judges arrive.

into the pen with the cat. You must have water in the bowl at all times – some people bring their own bottled still water – and check the cat regularly. The rules even state when you are allowed to place food in the cat's pen. Toys are often only allowed after judging has finished.

Depending on the individual show style, either the judges go around the pens or the cats are taken to a judging arena where they are assessed. In Britain, the owners often have to

leave their animals while they are judged. In Europe and America, however, owners remain in an inner showing square formed by the cat pens, and can be quite close to the judging table, while the rest of the public mill around outside the square.

The winners of each class are either announced or posted on a results board. At many shows the best cat in show is selected from the class winners by a panel of judges.

Finally, it is time to make a fuss of your long-suffering animal – whether it has won anything or not – and then head for home.

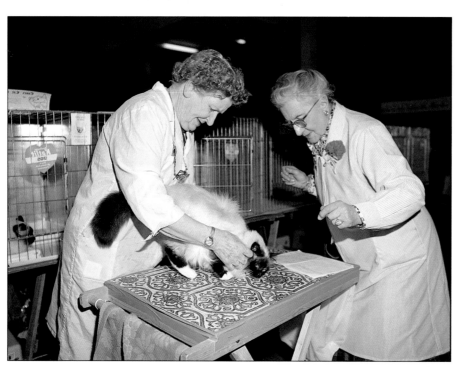

◆ TOP
Pens can be rather austere, but you can put in a favourite blanket, a litter tray (pan), and most important of all, a bowl of water.

◆ ABOVE FAR LEFT
Neighbourly relations can sometimes become a little strained in the confined conditions at a cat show.

◆ ABOVE LEFT
An owner visits her cat after judging to keep it company. You should check your cat regularly during the course of the show.

◆ LEFT
Judges take the cats on to a judging table. They wipe their hands with disinfectant between handling each animal, to make sure germs are not carried from one animal to the other.

WHAT THE JUDGES LOOK FOR

The judges check each pedigreed cat against the standard of points for its breed that have been set by the show's governing body. (These standards of points are published and can be bought from the relevant organizations.) A maximum mark is set for each aspect of the cat to be judged, such as the head, tail or coat. This will vary according to the breed and will often differ slightly between one registering body and another. For example, a perfectly textured and coloured coat of an Abyssinian cat could earn 40 points and ideal eyes 5 points, whereas on a Siamese the eyes rate more highly at 20 points, and the coat is worth 35 points. If you want to ask a judge about your cat, it is fine to approach them on the day after judging has finished. Judges are almost certainly very successful breeders in their own right and have a lot of sound advice to give; don't dismiss them just because they have not given a high award to your cat. Contrary to popular belief, judges hate down-marking exhibits.

♦ BELOW
Here is an example of what judges would be looking for in a Blue-mitted Ragdoll under GCCF standards. They will also check the coat colour and pattern against the particular requirements for the breed, which in this case are worth 20 points.

TAIL (*5 points*)
Long, bushy, slightly tapered towards the tip. Should at least reach the shoulder and be in proportion to the body.

COAT
LENGTH, TEXTURE AND CONDITION
(*10 points*)
Silky texture, dense, and medium in length; ruff and knickerbockers preferred on mature cats; short summer coat is acceptable.
COLOUR AND MARKINGS (*20 points*)

HEAD (*20 points*)
Broad with flat plane, not domed, and width between the ears. Well-developed cheeks; rounded, well-developed muzzle; firm chin with level bite. Nose of medium length with a gentle dip, and slightly retroussé at the tip.

EARS (*5 points*)
Medium in size, set wide with a slight tilt forward. Should be well furnished and rounded at the tip.

EYES
(*10 points*)
Large, well opened, slightly oblique and set well apart. Blue in colour, the deeper the better.

LEGS AND
PAWS
(*10 points*)
Medium in length and substantial of bone; paws large, round, firm and tufted.

BODY AND NECK
(*20 points*)
Long and muscular body with broad chest; short, heavy-set neck.

THE BRITISH SHOW SCENE

Anonymity is carefully guarded in the United Kingdom; there is little of the conviviality of the European or North American judging arenas, or the flamboyance of the decorated pens. At judging time, the owners are banished from the show hall and the judges visit each cat in turn. No identifying features are allowed on the pens, and all visible equipment in the pen must be white—the blankets, the water and food bowls, the litter tray (pan) (even the litter itself, if you are a perfectionist). Results are pinned on a line of hoardings, which becomes the most crowded part of the show for the rest of the day.

There are three levels of show in Britain. Exemption shows are usually run by individual clubs. They are relatively informal and friendly. There are no major qualifying awards available, and some of the Governing Council for the Cat Fancy (GCCF)

◆ LEFT
The equipment inside a pen at a British show must be white, from the cat's blanket to the litter tray (pan). However, now this Oriental Shorthair has been judged, he is allowed to have a toy in his pen.

rules are relaxed. Sanction shows are run according to the rules but no major awards are available. These are also organized by clubs but non-members can enter, and they are a good starting point for new exhibits.

Championship shows are strictly regulated and licensed by the GCCF. This is where qualifying awards, such as challenge certificates, for the

country's top cat show, the Supreme, can be gained. To be awarded a challenge certificate, a cat – which must be an un-neutered adult over nine months old – must win its open class and then be "challenged" against the set standard of points to see if it is good enough for the certificate to be awarded. A cat awarded three challenge certificates from three different judges qualifies for championship status and can enter classes for champions only. There is a parallel process for neutered adult cats aiming for premier certificates and premier status.

At shows run under the rules of the GCCF, judges make notes on every cat in the more important classes, including the open class, and write full reports, which are published in the specialist cat magazine, *Cats*.

At most shows the best adult, kitten and neuter of each breed is awarded Best of Breed. At some

◆ LEFT
At the GCCF Supreme Show the cats are penned in decorated pens, but taken to plain pens in judging rings, as shown, in order to be judged. These pens are disinfected thoroughly between cats.

◆ BELOW
The British owners have to take evidence
of their awards and collect their rosettes
from the rosette bench.

shows, especially the smaller specialist breed shows, Best in Show is held. Judges each nominate their best adult, kitten and neuter, and those nominated cats are judged against each other to select the Best in Show Adult, Kitten and Neuter and, often, the Best Exhibit in Show. When Best in Show is held at an all-breed show, the "Bests" are selected in each section – Longhair, Semi-longhair, British, Foreign, Burmese, Oriental and Siamese. The non-pedigreed cats also have their own Best in Show, but never compete against the pedigreed cats.

Open classes are open to all cats of a particular breed, regardless of whether they have previously won or not. They are split into male and female sections, neutered and entire cats, and kittens and adults.

There are also various miscellaneous classes for: cats bred by the exhibitor, cats under or over two years old, cats which have not yet won a first prize, and so on. Whether fun or serious, these classes give every exhibitor, however experienced, the opportunity to measure an exhibit's worth against the best of the rest; crucial if a serious show campaign is being planned. Most shows also have a section for non-pedigree cats.

If competition is not the aim, there is the possibility of placing the cat on exhibition. Here, the cat reclines in a splendidly decorated pen all day surrounded by evidence of past show glories. Often the full pedigree is on display and the cat does not have to face the indignity of being hauled out of the pen periodically.

The highest accolades for a British cat are won at the annual Supreme Cat Show. Here, judges provide a written

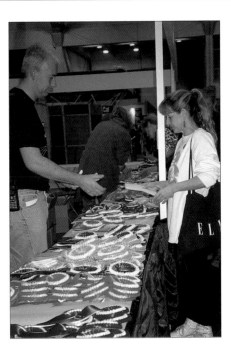

◆ BELOW
A pair of Persian Bi-colour youngsters destined for the show circuit.

resumé that the owners can see on the day. Only winners at lower-level championship shows are eligible to enter. The ultimate titles – Supreme Adult, Supreme Kitten and Supreme – are held for life. All three then compete for Supreme Exhibit.

SHOWING IN EIRE

Shows in the Republic of Ireland follow a similar style to that of the United Kingdom. The governing body is the Governing Council of the Cat Fancy in Ireland (GCCFI). Most judges are from the United Kingdom. Titles awarded to individual animals are ratified by the British organization. If a cat becomes a champion with both GCCF and GCCFI, it is granted the title International Champion.

EUROPEAN STYLE

Many European Shows last two days, as many exhibitors travel from other countries or even continents. The judges usually take different classes on the second day, so that wins gained on the first day are not duplicated on the second.

When quarantine regulations are relaxed, it may be possible for animals to have access to the full range of European cat shows, but they will have to be suitably vaccinated and micro-chipped. Certain differences in show style between Britain and the rest of Europe, however, will probably continue.

European shows are generally organized either by Fifé (*Fédération Internationale Féline*) or one of the independent clubs. Fifé, founded in 1949, is not just a European organization but has member states throughout the world, excluding, however, the United States, Canada, Australia, New Zealand and Japan.

There has traditionally been a sound working relationship between Fifé and the British GCCF, although each organization continues to retain much of its independence in decision-making and rules. Europe's numerous independent cat clubs operate as autonomous federations with their own registries, but cooperate and usually accept exhibitors from other clubs at their shows.

Some of the shows run by independent clubs have two different judging methods going on at the same time. After vetting-in, the cats are penned, sometimes with other entries from the same household, in a large show pen which may be sumptuously decorated with pedigrees, photographs, previous wins and cattery cards on display. The show pens are often arranged in squares, with the exhibitors inside the square having access to the animals, and the outward-facing side protected with perspex or heavy polythene so that the animals cannot be touched by the visitors on the outside of the square. Within the square of pens it is common for tables to be set up and laden with food and drink, so that the exhibitors can have a good day with their friends. It is very convivial.

Every cat is given a written report on how it conforms to the standard on that day, with the following ratings:

♦ *Excellent:* indicates that the animal has no physical defects; it conforms to standard; and is worthy of being bred from.
♦ *Very good:* indicates a cat of lesser quality relative to its standard of points, which is not good enough to gain a certificate.
♦ *Good:* indicates several defects or falling short of required standard.

All the cats are then judged for each award or qualification, and finally, Best in Section and Best in Show awards are decided.

♦ ABOVE
In European and North American shows, pens can be elaborately decorated, although at British shows, only cats "on exhibition" or at the Supreme Show, as shown, can rest in splendour such as this.

♦ LEFT
European Shorthairs have to reach the desired general standards of points rather than display a full pedigree to be eligible.

SHOWING IN AMERICA

♦ LEFT
Maine Coon Cats
were major
competitors at the
very first American
cat show held in
Madison Square
Garden, New York,
in 1895.

Most shows in the United States, Mexico and Canada are full weekend occasions; some may even extend to three days. There may not be a preliminary vetting, on the assumption that no honourable exhibitor would take a sick animal to a show.

The holding pens at an American show are arranged like those in Europe, within a square (known as the ring) enclosed by the cages of the exhibitors. The owners can stay within the ring with their cats, and be fairly close to the judges when they give their verdict. The general public is on the outside of the square, and the outward-facing sides of the pens are usually protected from poking hands by heavy plastic sheets.

The judges remove each cat entrant in turn from its pen, to make an assessment against the required standards, accompanied by a simultaneous commentary. In virtually all North American associations, the judge is able to comment only on the favourable aspects of the animal, and not the negative points. Apart from brief notes for personal use, the judges make no written assessment of the cats.

At the end of the show, the ten top kittens, adults and neuters in the Longhair, Shorthair and All Breed sections are taken to the ring for the Best Cat award. The placements are announced starting at tenth and working upwards. They are important, for promotion to championship status in the American system depends not only on points scored in class wins, but on how many top five placements in the Best Cat stakes have been gained. It is not unknown, though rare, for a cat to become a Grand Champion at its very first show. There are classes for

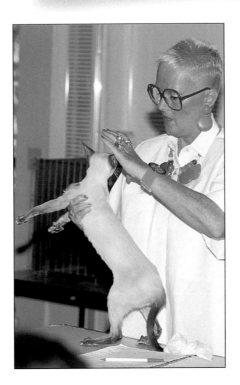

♦ ABOVE
American judges often keep up a running commentary on the good points of each cat as they are assessing the animals.

♦ RIGHT
This mixed breed Dilute Calico Van is a top award-winning American cat. Most shows have classes for non-pedigrees. The cats are judged on general appearance, condition and temperament rather than on specific points.

unaltered, pedigreed cats over eight months old, kitten competitions for animals of four to eight months, and provisional classes for breeds that have not been granted championship status (that is, registered as a distinct breed) by the registering association.

Various associations in North America promote the "campaigning" of the very top cats. Exhibitors fly and drive huge distances to attend the shows where the greatest concentration of top cats will be found. Points are scored at every show attended in pursuit of championship or premiership status. The ultimate award is that of National Top Cat. Even to get into the National Top Twenty-five is a remarkable achievement.

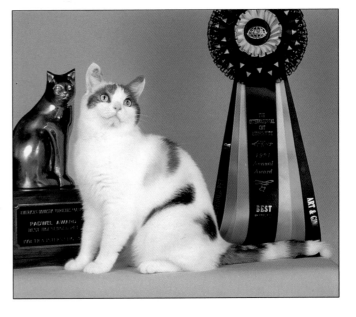

GLOSSARY

agouti a coat pattern where each individual hair is banded with two or three different colours.

albino a genetic term referring to a lack of pigmentation in the skin and hair, resulting in an abnormally white animal with pink eyes.

applehead describes a flattened head shape, usually referring to the old-fashioned Siamese.

back-cross the process of mating a cat to one of its own forebears, sometimes including its parent.

bi-colour a white cat with solid patches of another colour in its coat.

breed a particular and consistent type, colour and size of cat that is officially registered by one of the cat associations.

brindled where there are hairs of a different colour, usually white, in a solid coloured part of the coat. This can be particularly noticeable on the mask of a Seal Point Siamese.

calico American term for a tortoiseshell and white cat.

cameo describes a white or silver coat that is subtly **tipped** with red, cream or with tortoiseshell.

Cat Fancy the selective breeding and exhibiting of cats.

chinchilla a white cat whose coat has the lightest form of tipping, with dark tips at the very top of each hair shaft.

chintz another term for a **calico** or tortoiseshell and white cat.

cobby describes a short-legged, sturdy-bodied build.

Colourpoint longhaired cat of Persian type with a restricted **Himalayan** coat pattern. The American term for the Colourpoint Persian is **Himalayan**.

colourpointed any breed of cat, other than Siamese and Colourpoint Persian (Himalayan) that displays the restricted **Himalayan** points.

dilute a genetic term referring to a paler version of a basic, **dominant** dark coat colour, for example, the dilute version of black is blue.

dominant 1. the base colour of a breed, which is usually black or brown; 2. genetic term for a gene that over-rides another, so that its particular characteristics are expressed in the carrier's offspring.

Foreign a term to describe a cat of more elongated type compared to **cobby** British or Persian type.

genotype the genetic make-up of a cat, as distinct from the outward appearance (see also **phenotype**).

guardhairs the topcoat of fur over the awn (undercoat) and soft down hairs. Not all cats have all three levels.

heat see **oestrus**.

Himalayan 1. the American term for a Colourpoint Persian; 2. a genetic characteristic expressed in dark points on ears, face, legs and tail on an otherwise pale-coated cat.

mask the facial marking of a cat.

nose leather the leather-like nose area.

oestrus term describing the state of a female cat on heat or in season, when she is sexually receptive.

Oriental cats typified by long limbs, svelte bodies, a wedge-shaped face, almond eyes and pointed ears.

parti-colour one or more colours or patterns on a white coat, as in tortoiseshell and white.

pedigree a written record of a cat's ancestry, showing its parentage over several generations.

peke-faced an American term used to describe a Persian Longhair with a very short-nosed, flat face.

Persian longhaired cat of Persian type, quite distinct from the members of the semi-longhaired group.

phenotype the outward, physical appearance of a cat, as distinct from the genetic make-up, or **genotype**, which is often quite different.

points the cat's face, ears, lower legs and tail, which may in some cases be a darker colour than the main body as in the **Colourpoint** or Siamese.

prefix a name registered by a breeder and placed before any particular name of an individual cat, denoting the breeding line of the cattery.

queen a female cat, over nine months of age, that has not been spayed and is capable of breeding when she is in **oestrus** or on heat.

recessive gene a gene that, on its own, is usually over-ridden by the **dominant** gene and therefore not expressed in physical characteristics. Two such genes, one from each parent, must be present in a kitten for the characteristic caused by this gene to be displayed. Examples of recessive genes are those for blue or chocolate coat colour.

rex describes a coat that is curled or crinkled, as seen in the Cornish Rex and Devon Rex breeds.

ruff the distinctive longer fur as seen around the neck of many semi-longhaired cats.

self a solid-coloured cat with no pattern or shading in the coat.

shaded a **tipped** coat, midway between the **chinchilla** and the **smoke**.

smoke the effect of the inhibitor (silver) gene on a non-**agouti** coat. Each hair is dark for 30–60 per cent of its length and silver at the base.

solid see **self**.

standard of points the standards of size, colouring, markings and other characteristics for pedigreed breeds that are laid down by the cat-registrating bodies. Judges assess each cat against the standard of points for its particular breed.

tabby striped, blotched, spotted or ticked markings that in the wild give the optical illusion of breaking up body shape as a form of camouflage.

ticked 1. when applied to hairs, another term for **agouti**; 2. when applied to pattern, the **tabby** pattern as seen in an Abyssian cat.

tipped the colouring of a cat's fur at the very tip of each hair shaft, the remainder of the fur being pale.

torbie an abbreviation used for tortoiseshell-tabby.

tortie an abbreviation for tortoiseshell.

tri-colour another term for **calico**, **chintz** or tortoiseshell and white.

type the ideal head and body shape of a cat as laid down in the **standard of points**.

van a type of coat pattern consisting of a white body with a coloured tail and coloured spots on the head.

INDEX

ACKNOWLEDGEMENTS

The publishers would like to thank Paddy Cutts for her invaluable help.

The photographer and publishers would like to thank the following for their assistance with the photography: Paddy Cutts, Alison Hay, S. and R. Badger, S. Bagley, G. Black, V. Dyer, C. Fry, Wade and Kirby Heames, H. Hewitt, B. Hollandt, J. and D. Johnson, R. Lowen, B. and L. Riddy, Pampered Pets, Colin Clark veterinary practice, Burntwood boarding cattery, Weycolour Ltd.
Persian: S. McHale, Isabella Bans, Lynn Lincoln, Jo and Nick Bolton, Maxine Fothergill, Carol Gainsbury, Rose Lovelidge.
Turkish Van: T. Burnstone, Joyce Johnson. **Somali:** Jane Bean, Celestine Hanley, Rosie Lowen. **Maine Coon Cat:** Mr and Mrs Badger, Daphne Butters, Sue Deane, Bill Griffiths, Jackie Huddlestone. **Norwegian Forest Cat:** Ginny Black, Pete and Ann Bowler, Pat Stewart. **Balinese:** Mrs P. Browning, Mr and Mrs Cleland, Luisa Jones, Mr and Mrs Meerings, Mrs Pinnington.
British Angora: Ian Connerton.
Ragdoll: Belinda Bright, Dawn Davies, Janet Edwards, Dianne Mackey. **Tiffanie:** Cindy Matthews, Jennifer Ray.
Cymric: A. and J. Beresford.
Exotic: Mr and Mrs J. Clark, Rosemary Fisher, Maxine Fothergill, Carol Gainsbury, Shelagh Heavens. **British Shorthair:** Brenda Hollandt, Paulette Larmour, Celia Leighton. **European Shorthair:** Stephanie Cole. **Oriental Shorthair:** Carolyn Fry, Mr and Mrs Funnell, Monica Harcourt, Sheena Manchline, Betty Winyard. **Siamese:** E. Corps, Sheena Manchline, Lynn Studer, B. Reece. **Snowshoe:** Mrs M. Shackell. **Seychellois:** Barbara Lambert. **Abyssinian:** Cindy Bailey, Ann Curtis, Mrs H. Hewitt, Heather Reay. **Russian Blue:** Val Price. **Korat:** Judith Jewkes, Jen Lacey. **Burmese:** Maria Chapman, Dr. Kim Jarvis, Naomi Johnson, Mrs Marriott Power, Mr and Mrs P. Webb, S. Williams-Ellis. **Burmilla:** Mrs C. Clarke. **Asian:** Mrs P. Impson, Deborah Laugher, Jennie Quiddington, Michelle Robinson. **Bengal:** Sandra Bush, Helen Hewitt. **Tonkinese:** Hazel Forshore, Carol Poole, Linda Vousden. **Singapura:** Debbie van den Berg. **Ocicat:** L. Abbs, R. Caunter, V. Phillips. **Manx:** A. and J. Beresford. **Cornish Rex:** S. Luxford Watts. **Devon Rex:** Stephanie Cole, Chris Franks. **Sphynx:** Maureen Roddick. **Non-pedigree:** Monica Harcourt.

The publishers acknowledge reference to the Standard of Points booklet published by The Governing Council of the Cat Fancy, 4-6 Penel Orlieu, Bridgwater, TA6 3PG.